A SELF-DEVELOPMENT PROGRAMME

Effective delegation

THE ESSENTIAL GUIDE TO THINKING AND WORKING SMARTER

Chris Roebuck

MARSHALL PUBLISHING • LONDON

A Marshall Edition
Conceived, edited and
designed by
Marshall Editions Ltd
The Orangery
161 New Bond Street
London W1Y 9PA

First published in the UK
in 1998 by
Marshall Publishing Ltd

Copyright © 1998
Marshall Editions
Developments Ltd

ISBN 1-84028-134-0

Series Consultant Editor
Chris Roebuck
Project Editor
Conor Kilgallon
Design
Strukture Design
Art Director
Sean Keogh
Managing Art Editor
Patrick Carpenter
Managing Editor
Clare Currie
Editorial Assistant
Sophie Sandy
Editorial Coordinator
Becca Clunes
Production
Nikki Ingram
Cover Design
Poppy Jenkins

Originated in Italy by
Articolor
Printed and bound in
France by SIRC

Video Arts quotes extracted from training films:

pp 9, 10, 28, 34, 41: "The Unorganised Manager Pt 1 & 2"

...ed on or be... ...mped below

A SELF...VELO...NT PROGRAMME

Effective delegation

Acknowledgements

The following organizations and individuals have
contributed to the preparation of this book or to the
development of the approaches taken in it:
Jeremy & Lindsay McTeague
Paul Hersey & Kenneth Blanchard
Dr Paul Dobson – City University Business School
Colonel Ian Rodley – 1st Royal Tank Regiment
City University Business School
Royal Military Academy Sandhurst
Army Junior Division, Joint Service Command
    & Staff College
MaSt Organisation
John McBride & Nick Clark

Contents

1

The importance of delegation
The benefits of improving skills
How do you delegate at present?

Maximising your time

Maximising team performance

Motivating and developing your team

Improving your leadership skills

Why do you need to delegate effectively?

Even outside work everyone regularly uses delegation skills in all areas of life – should you enlist a friend to repair the car, can the children clean their rooms, shall you bring in a tradesman to fix the broken door handle? You make such decisions on a daily basis, even if you are not a manager; these are all delegation decisions. So being effective at delegation has benefits in many areas, some not related to work.

What is delegation?

Delegation is the allocation of jobs to individuals or teams. Effective delegation gives the jobs to the people who are best suited to do them and then gives them the right degree of freedom to perform the job in the most efficient and productive way.

Effective delegation allows you, and your whole team, to perform at your best and develop to face new challenges. With poor delegation the team is constantly engaged in "firefighting" and wastes valuable time. The team will not be performing at its best and will probably not be able to develop skills necessary to meet any future challenges.

Delegation is never static – as the jobs that your team do change, how you delegate must adapt as well. Also, people change and develop with time and how you delegate to those individuals must alter as they do. Being able to delegate is a key skill for all those with responsibility for others – indeed for anyone who has to get other people to do tasks for them.

Recognizing skills

It is not just those new to management or supervisory jobs who find difficulty in delegating; many senior managers still have a problem with "letting go". They can forget that, while someone might have been inexperienced five years ago, by now their knowledge and experience have developed so they can take on more responsibility.

You know from your own experience that a boss who does not recognize that you have developed and gained more skills by giving you more responsibility can be a real hindrance. You get frustrated and demotivated – your potential is not being realized. This is one of the main complaints about bosses on all levels – "he doesn't give me the chance to show what I can do", or "what's the point in learning new skills if I'm not allowed to use them?". Make sure you don't do this to your team – use effective delegation to make sure that they are given more responsibility as their skills grow. If you're not sure what work they are able to take on you can always ask!

As well as just "getting the job done" effective delegation also has benefits in other areas that makes your life easier and improves team performance.

Improving time management

Delegation is probably the most important of all the time management skills, maximizing your time by passing on those tasks that others can do. You cannot do it all by yourself – the pressure of work for many people is now so high that, in reality, you have to delegate to survive. Many of you will think that you delegate all the jobs that you can, but studies have shown that most people who delegate could, in practical terms, delegate 10 percent more tasks than they currently do. Does 10 percent more time – over a month or a year – sound good to you?

Improving team motivation

How and what you delegate is also important for your team members; it shows them how much you trust them and what you think of their abilities. If you delegate to them it confirms that you trust their approach to work and shows that you recognize and value their talents by giving them the responsibility – and you motivate them in the process. So as well as being inefficient, poor delegation can demotivate your team; if you don't delegate, individuals feel their skills and knowledge are not valued by you.

Improving team development

Via effective delegation you can develop your team. By giving them tasks that are right on the limit of their capabilities, or even just beyond, you can encourage them to develop their skills and knowledge. This may be by giving them a job that you would normally do but which with support they could undertake. This will help you, as next time they can do the job themselves, giving you more time to concentrate on those tasks that only you can do. As new technology and systems are introduced, it is important that your team develop skills in new areas. Effective delegation is key to this ongoing process.

...with delegation you take your hands off but keep your eyes open...

Will improving your skills bring benefits?

...you can't delegate a new job without proper training...

Effective delegation is one of the critical components of effective leadership – so if you can get your delegation skills right you will probably also be performing well in a major part of your managerial role.

The benefits of effective delegation are:

- Maximizing your time resources to allow you time for the tasks you should be doing.
- Giving each task to the person or team best suited to it.
- Effectively using the experts who have knowledge that you don't have.
- Helping the individual or team develop new skills and enhance knowledge.
- Motivating the team more – because they are being given responsibility and are trusted to get on with jobs.
- Enhancing your role as team leader – by the improvement in team performance and demon-strated by the extra responsibility you have given to people.
- Improving your leadership skills.

At this point it is worth being clear on the first rule of delegating:

"You can delegate all the job but you can't delegate all the responsibility." This worries some people just in case things go wrong, but if you delegate effectively the job should go according to plan – and the consequences of not delegating are even worse.

The dangers of not delegating effectively are:

- Spending too much time supervising others and not having time for your own work.
- Not allocating jobs to the person or team best suited to them – so they either don't get done or take longer than they should.
- Ineffective use of team skills or expertise – not using specialist knowledge of experts.
- The team, and individuals, not developing new skills or extending their knowledge.
- The team, and individuals within it, becoming demotivated because they are not being given the responsibility they both want and can accept.

Thinking about how you delegate

As you can see, and as you can probably confirm from your experience the effects of delegation extend into areas that underpin the whole viability of the team as an effective unit. On a strategic level, the performance of the multitude of teams within the organisation combines to determine the performance of the organisation. So the overall costs of poor delegation can be substantial, as can be the benefits of good delegation. Don't forget that in the end this boils down to the bottom line – financial performance. Ineffective organisations go bust.

Lack of training

Despite the importance of making sure that everybody in charge of a team is good at delegating, many organisations don't even bother to offer any training on how to do it! They presume that you will learn it by some form of telepathy, or by trial and error. The problem is that most people aren't telepathic and the error part of trial and error wastes both time and resources. So despite the potential costs and loss of benefits, your organisation will probably not have given you any help in developing your delegation skills – and this applies to senior managers as well!

Provided you adopt a positive approach to developing your skills and work hard to get it right in practice, you will find that you can quickly develop your skills. So you now have no need for telepathy and for you the error element in trial and error will be much reduced – by virtue of the combination of your experience and this book.

To be effective at delegating the critical questions you need to answer are:
- Which jobs should I delegate?
- Who should I delegate the different jobs to?
- How should I tell them what I want done?
- How should I make sure it gets done?

If you have absolutely no problems in answering all the questions above when you have work to be done then your delegation skills may be excellent. But the majority of managers, even if they have a good idea of what to do in principle, tend not to implement it as well as they could in practice. This book will help you understand how to be effective when delegating by giving you simple formats that will enable you to get it right in situations you are likely to meet at work.

Thinking about how you delegate

From principle to practice

The transition from principle to practice is always difficult. If the pressure at work was low, all the work came in on time, there were no rush jobs, deadlines didn't change, bosses and team members didn't alter and you had time to think, then it would be easy. Unfortunately, life isn't like that, and you have to delegate in a pressurized and constantly changing environment.

It can seem complicated and confusing, particularly if you are new to delegating. There are, however, simple ways to make the process easy in practice and of helping you to be effective at delegating in most of the situations you are likely to meet.

So which jobs do you delegate? Have you ever thought about why you delegate some jobs and not others? Is there some formula that you can use to aid your decision? One way to help you start is for you to write down three of the jobs you delegate to others and three which you do yourself. Next to each write why you delegate or do that job yourself. Look over the answers and see if there is a pattern of factors that determine why you hand over some jobs and keep others. If there is, what mix of factors makes you delegate and what combination do the job yourself?

You can analyse why you allocate different jobs to different people in the same way. Write down six jobs you delegate and beside each enter the reason why you delegate this job to this person. Is there a pattern of common factors that you consider when delegating?

Having decided that you want to delegate a job and who you want to allocate it to, how do you tell them what you want them to do? Does it vary for jobs involving one person or more than one person? Do you brief them in a formal or informal way? What information do you need to give someone you are delegating to? This is important – just briefly jot down the type of information you normally give to people when you delegate to them.

Having delegated the job to someone, how much freedom do you give them to get on with it? Do you explain in specific detail or just tell them what you want achieved at the end? Would you give different people differing levels of freedom for the same job? Write down two jobs your team does where the amount of freedom you give to the person doing the job varies according to who is doing it. Why does your degree of freedom vary – what is the critical factor in this decision?

Write down three jobs that you delegate and three that you do yourself. Why do you delegate them or do them yourself? Is there a common factor?

1 _____

2 _____

3 _____

4 _____

5 _____

6 _____

By reading through this book and using the approaches in it you will be able to see how you are doing at present. You will then be introduced to proven methods of getting delegation right and be able to use these to develop your skills in the future.

You may also be able to use the knowledge you gain in this process to develop your team. This book can be of ongoing value to you – you can regularly use the contents, particularly the self-assessments, to tell how you have improved and put together development plans for the future.

If you use all the ideas in the book you will find that work becomes more enjoyable because delegation becomes a pleasure not a pain.

**Critical Points - Chapter 1
Effective delegation:**

■ **Maximizes the time you have for the jobs you need to do.**
■ **Maximizes team performance.**
■ **Motivates and develops your team.**
■ **Improves your leadership skills.**

Everyone can improve their delegation skills with a little thought and practice.

2

How good are your skills now?
Do you delegate effectively?
Your preferred delegation style

Assessing your own skills

Delegation in general

Specific areas at work

Assessing your delegation skills

efore you can develop your skills in any area you need to know how good they are at present. This is important as it will enable you to concentrate your efforts where they require the most improvement. You have already written a few notes on how you handle delegation with your team in the previous chapter. Chapter 2 is designed to build on that first step by taking you through a general self-assessment process. By the end of it you will be able to identify your strengths and weaknesses and then be able to plan how to improve your skills.

You first need to assess whether you delegate enough and then to discover if you delegate in the most effective way. To do this you should answer the questions on the following pages. At the end of each section you can analyse your answers.

Statement	5	4	3	2	1	Statement
1a I believe it is important to delegate a task that may be at the limit of a team member's current abilities.						**1b** I delegate tasks that I don't like doing myself and never delegate anything unless I am sure that others can handle it.
2a I assess a person's strengths and weaknesses before delegating a project and make sure they have the backup they need.						**2b** I would delegate far more if I felt that my team members could handle it.
3a I could usually do tasks that I delegate more quickly myself but what I delegate is not crucial to my current job priorities.						**3b** If I can do something myself I usually do so, even if it means another key task is postponed.
4a I think others learn most effectively through doing a variety of jobs. I am pleased when a member of my team takes a better position in the organization or elsewhere.						**4b** I would like to give team members opportunities for advancement but there is seldom any time to do so.
5a I never do anything that can be handled by somebody on my team.						**5b** I often do trivial tasks.

Do you delgate effectively at present?

This questionnaire is designed to give a general assessment of your delegation skills. Put a tick in the box nearest the statement that best represents your approach. So, for instance, if your approach is halfway between the two put the tick in the middle box. Then add the figures up for each box you have ticked: the values are at the top of each. This gives you your total – see how you did by reading the table below the quiz.

Statement		5	4	3	2	1		Statement
6a	I always plan delegation in advance, knowing what to delegate and who will be given a project ahead of time.						**6b**	I delegate as and when it becomes necessary to whoever has the lightest workload at the time.
7a	Before delegating a task I think about what should be achieved, how the task should be done and how long it should take. Where possible I agree this with the person doing the job beforehand.						**7b**	I always give objectives, the way I want the work done and when it has to be done by when I tell them they have the job.
8a	I think regular updates on how delegated work is going are vital and I set up times for progress reports at the start of the project.						**8b**	I call people in to discuss progress on tasks only if I have some spare time.
9a	I always stick to a 'hands off' approach on jobs until the agreed review date/time.						**9b**	I step in at once if I hear or suspect a delegated job may not be going right.
10a	At the end of a project I think a review of what was done and how is vital.						**10b**	Making time for reviews is not important – after all the job's done.

How did you score?

More than 45

Your delegation skills appear to be good. Those in your team should have a fair idea of what you want and when you want it done. However, there may be one or two parts in which you did not score 5 – you may want to improve these slightly weaker areas.

35–44

Your delegation skills are reasonable but in some areas development can make them even better. Consider the areas where your scores were lower – these are where you should try to improve.

What does this tell you?

Unless you scored 50, there is scope to improve your delegation skills. Run back through your statements: the first five show your attitude to delegating to your team, the second five how you do it in practice. The best score for each pair of statements is a five, so the lower the score the weaker you are in this area. What the best approach or action is for each question is indicated by the left-hand statement.

25–34

While you have some skills in this area you can achieve considerable improvement in your performance, and that of your team, by spending time developing skills in the areas in which you are weak.

15–24

Your delegation skills are not good and you need to make a concerted effort to improve them. It is probable that your team is not performing as well as it could, as a direct result of your weakness in this area.

10–14

Your skills need substantial improvement in many areas. Your team is almost certainly underperforming because your delegation skills are poor. They are not being given the jobs they are capable of. You are probably spending much more time than you should on jobs you could get the team to do.

What is your preferred delegation style?

Many people tend to delegate in a similar way on most occasions: for example, at one extreme, the manager who retains tight control of all jobs and, at the other, someone who gives full responsibility to the team when they can't really handle it. You can probably think of examples of both these types that you have worked with. They tend to use this one approach, or style, of delegating whatever the situation.

There are other styles: this next questionnaire is designed to help you see which delegation styles you use most. It does this by looking at how you approach a number of areas critical to effective delegation: setting objectives, motivating, communicating and performance evaluation/feedback. Armed with this knowledge you can then plan how to make your delegation style as effective as possible.

Read the statements over the page relating to delegation. They are in groups of four (1–4, 5–8, 9–12 and so on). Then score yourself for each set of four by choosing which of the statements is most similar to the way you think or act; give this "4" points. Award the next most similar to you "3" points, the one after "2" points and the one that is least like the way you think or act "1" point. For example, if in the first set (1–4) you feel that number 3 is most similar to the way you think or act then circle the "4" box beside statement 3. If 1 is next most similar to you circle the "3" box beside statement 1 and so on to the choice that is least similar to what you think or do, where you circle box "1" beside the relevant statement.

Delegation style scoring system	
Most similar	4 points
Second most similar	3 points
Next most similar	2 points
Least similar	1 point

Questionnaire

Telling them how to do the job

1 It is important to explain the task clearly to the person doing the job.

| 4 | 3 | 2 | 1 |

2 I believe I should tell people exactly what I want accomplished.

| 4 | 3 | 2 | 1 |

3 I give my team the freedom to set their own detailed objectives.

| 4 | 3 | 2 | 1 |

4 I tend to give my team a general outline of what I want and let them get on with it.

| 4 | 3 | 2 | 1 |

5 People don't understand what I really want.

| 4 | 3 | 2 | 1 |

6 Sometimes I'm told I'm being slightly too directive when setting tasks.

| 4 | 3 | 2 | 1 |

7 I always tell people precisely what they have to do and how they have to do it.

| 4 | 3 | 2 | 1 |

8 I sometimes feel that my team may be unsure about what to do.

| 4 | 3 | 2 | 1 |

Working together

9 I wish my people could develop ways of working more as a "team".

4 | 3 | 2 | 1

10 I tell my team that they should work effectively with each other.

4 | 3 | 2 | 1

11 I tell each team member the role I want them to play.

4 | 3 | 2 | 1

12 I encourage the team to meet regularly to share ideas.

4 | 3 | 2 | 1

13 I sometimes don't give my team members enough freedom to help each other.

4 | 3 | 2 | 1

14 Too much time is wasted discussing issues without coming to any useful conclusions.

4 | 3 | 2 | 1

15 I sometimes spend too much time with each individual to allow enough time for the whole team to be together.

4 | 3 | 2 | 1

16 The team is sometimes so busy with a whole range of different jobs that I feel they're becoming a group of individuals.

4 | 3 | 2 | 1

Most similar
4 points

Second most similar
3 points

Next most similar
2 points

Least similar
1 point

Questionnaire

Keeping in touch with what's going on

17 I tell everyone what they need to know – no more, no less. But I expect them to tell me exactly what is happening.

| 4 | 3 | 2 | 1 |

18 I like to give team members the chance to tell me how things are going if they want.

| 4 | 3 | 2 | 1 |

19 I regularly tell my team what is going on so they understand where I'm coming from.

| 4 | 3 | 2 | 1 |

20 I always like taking time out to ask team members how everything's going.

| 4 | 3 | 2 | 1 |

21 Sometimes I find out about problems too late to do anything about them.

| 4 | 3 | 2 | 1 |

22 I think team members feel they cannot raise delicate or awkward matters with me.

| 4 | 3 | 2 | 1 |

23 In many cases I don't know what my team thinks about jobs we are involved in.

| 4 | 3 | 2 | 1 |

24 I've noticed that I can get sidetracked talking to the team and listen to them but not pass on any information myself.

| 4 | 3 | 2 | 1 |

Motivating my team

25 If I work very closely with my team on jobs this will motivate them more.

| 4 | 3 | 2 | 1 |

26 I think that if I give my team more freedom of action this motivates them more.

| 4 | 3 | 2 | 1 |

27 I encourage the team to come up with ideas to motivate themselves more.

| 4 | 3 | 2 | 1 |

28 When discussing job performance I don't beat about the bush; I tell them straight what I think about them.

| 4 | 3 | 2 | 1 |

29 When I deal with my team I take no notice of how individuals are motivated.

| 4 | 3 | 2 | 1 |

30 If necessary I will put a lot of pressure on my team to achieve results.

| 4 | 3 | 2 | 1 |

31 Occasionally I spend too much time talking to my team about their views.

| 4 | 3 | 2 | 1 |

32 The best performers in my team need to be able to motivate themselves.

| 4 | 3 | 2 | 1 |

Most similar
4 points

Second most similar
3 points

Next most similar
2 points

Least similar
1 point

Questionnaire

Keeping the job on track

33 If an individual's performance is not too good I like to discuss and agree solutions to the problems.

4 | 3 | 2 | 1

34 If I work very closely with my team it helps keep everything on track.

4 | 3 | 2 | 1

35 If things aren't going well I act quickly and firmly to put them right.

4 | 3 | 2 | 1

36 I think it is down to individuals and the team as a whole to maintain their own high standards.

4 | 3 | 2 | 1

37 When it comes to chasing up poor performance I am often fairly relaxed about it.

4 | 3 | 2 | 1

38 I can't understand why team members don't take responsibility for their own work standards.

4 | 3 | 2 | 1

39 I find it hard to move from a supporting role to one in which I have deal with poor performance.

4 | 3 | 2 | 1

40 I may be a little hard on people who don't perform to the standards I want.

4 | 3 | 2 | 1

Helping them to do the job

41 I think it important to let the team know what development plans I have for them.

| 4 | 3 | 2 | 1 |

42 The best way to make people feel support is available is to have regular discussions of team activities.

| 4 | 3 | 2 | 1 |

43 I try to keep closely in touch with team members so that I can ask them about their problems.

| 4 | 3 | 2 | 1 |

44 I encourage my team to feel that I am available at any time if they need help.

| 4 | 3 | 2 | 1 |

45 Occasionally I spend too much effort on being nice to everyone in my team.

| 4 | 3 | 2 | 1 |

46 I should let my team learn more from their experience rather than being too over-protective.

| 4 | 3 | 2 | 1 |

47 I often think that I may be too distant from my team.

| 4 | 3 | 2 | 1 |

48 Few of my team would come to me with their problems.

| 4 | 3 | 2 | 1 |

Most similar
4 points

Second most similar
3 points

Next most similar
2 points

Least similar
1 point

Scoring your results

Now add up the scores for the following questions:							
Question	**Score**	**Question**	**Score**	**Question**	**Score**	**Question**	**Score**
2		1		4		3	
7		6		5		8	
11		10		12		9	
13		15		14		16	
17		19		20		18	
23		22		24		21	
28		25		27		26	
29		30		31		32	
35		34		33		36	
40		39		37		38	
41		43		42		44	
48		46		45		47	
Total		**Total**		**Total**		**Total**	
	Controller		**Coach**		**Consultant**		**Co-ordinator**

Plotting your scores

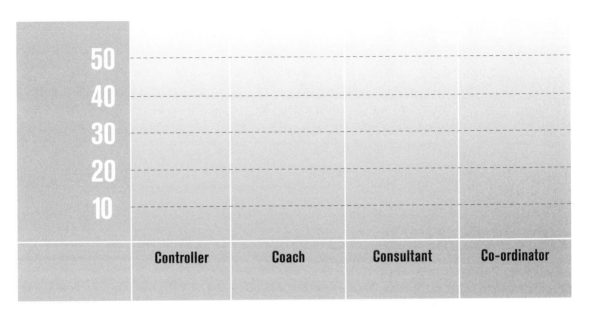

	50				
	40				
	30				
	20				
	10				
		Controller	Coach	Consultant	Co-ordinator

Now you have added up the scores on the previous page transfer the total for each to the graph on this page. Do this by making a column above the relevant style label so that the top of the column lines up with the score on the left. For exampe, if your "controller" score was 40, you would make the column go from the base line to the 40 level. Once you have completed the four columns, make a note of the which style scored the most points, down to the style that scored the least.

The peaks of the columns show which style of delegation you tend to use most; the troughs those you tend to use least. There is no "correct answer" to this questionnaire – it depends on the job you are doing, the team you work with and your personality.

However, there are general indicators that may help you assess your style. As you will see later, to be fully effective you need to develop the ability to use a range of delegation styles to match different situations.

So what does each mean?

Controller

Those who use the controller style to delegate want their own detailed plans carried out. They issue specific instructions and closely supervise the job. This may even mean telling the person carrying out the job what to do at each stage. They do not allow the person any freedom of action in how the job is carried out. Controllers may not explain why the task has to be done. The controller is often used where the person doing the job has little experience of that job and has to be told what to do at each stage. Some people use this style even for those who can do the job without close supervision. You should beware of this approach – it leads to demotivation!

Coach

Coaches closely supervise the task but generally take a less strictly directive approach. They explain about the task and take the person doing the job through it stage by stage, offering advice and support if they feel it is needed or when the boss thinks it should be given – proactive support. The important difference between the controller and the coach is that the person doing the task feels more responsible for the job and that they can input more themselves.

Consultant

The consultant gives even more freedom of action to the person doing the job. The task is outlined in a more general way and the delegator invites the person asked to do the work in hand for their ideas on how it should be done. Both then discuss the project and agree on a course of action. The person or team to which the task is delegated is required to supply much of the input. The delegator then makes clear that they will be available to provide further help and support should it be required. In this case it is expected that there may well be some need for this support, but it is generally given only when specifically requested – reactive support.

Co-ordinator/facilitator

The co-ordinator/facilitator gives an overall direction to the person doing the task but leaves the specifics to them. When delegating, the co-ordinator also agrees the level of freedom the person has before they must report back for further consultation. Generally, it is not expected that the person doing the job will need to seek support or advice during the task.

...you can't delegate until you've got yourself organised...

Summary

Each of these styles could be used in any situation. However, only one of them is the best to use in any particular set of circumstances. Effective delegation is the ability to correctly choose the style that matches the job in question with the person who is to do it.

Thus you should remember that different styles can be used for different jobs even when done by the same person. You will know people who are experienced at some jobs but new to others. It may be that the critical factor in the process is not WHO the person doing the job is, but how well they know the particular job you may have asked them to do. How does this bear out your experiences at work? List three people you know who are experienced at one job but less experienced at another one.

To some extent the results you have will reflect your job – if you are involved in the development of many inexperienced staff your "controller" rating may be high. If you have an expert and experienced team your "co-ordinator" rating may be highest.

Critical Points - Chapter 2

You will now have a good idea of your strengths and weaknesses as a delegator – write a rough list of each from what you have found out so far.
Remember the four delegation styles that people tend to use:

**CONTROLLER
COACH
CONSULTANT
CO-ORDINATOR**

Which style or styles do you use the most at work?
Have you thought why you use these styles when you do?

The critical question is whether the styles you are using match the situations you are in. You will see in the next chapter how to tell if you are getting it right and if you need to "tune" your approaches to delegating certain tasks or to certain people.

3

Delegation in practice
Delegation and motivation
Delegation problems

Steps to getting the job done

Determining objectives

Monitoring the job

Giving feedback

Delegation in practice

Having identified your general approach to delegation and the specific style you use, you can now move forward by looking at the process of delegation and how to get the job done in more detail. Your delegation has only been effective when the job is successfully completed. So to make sure this happens try answering the critical questions on the previous page.

If you have answers to all the questions and can implement them in practice then delegating a job should be a pleasure and not a worry. Run through the process of how you handle delegating jobs that might come in:

What exactly is the job I'm being asked to do?

While, strictly speaking, defining the job for yourself is not part of delegation, you need to make sure you are clear about what has to be done before you delegate it to anyone else. If it is a problem you are trying to solve this is especially true. Before delegating, you need to know that the job you delegate is going to have the effect you want. You can't complain if, when the job is done, it doesn't have the desired result if your directions have given the person misleading information. For example: *"I want you to reduce the flow of paper through the department, there's too much of the stuff and we're sinking under it."*

Does this mean get rid of the photocopier, introduce a computer-based information system, send a memo round telling people not to send so many memos round or decide which paper is important and which not? You can probably think of many cases like this of unclear directions – you need to make sure you know what is wanted.

This may seem to be irrelevant to delegating, but it is in fact critical. Many jobs go wrong not because the delegation was wrongly conducted, but because the task completed was not the one required to solve the problem.

The four stages

If you have a problem or are asked to do a job there are four stages you need to go through before you can decide if you are going to delegate and to whom. These are:

- Identify the precise problem or define exactly what you have been asked to do.
- Locate and analyse the cause of the problem or consider the different approaches to what you have been asked to do.
- Collect all the information you need on each potential option.
- Consider all the options and decide on the best one.

To make sure you are doing the right job and going to produce the best result you need to run through this process. Many people jump to one conclusion about what the best way to do a job is, but it then turns out not to be the solution. Also, just because it has been done this way before, doesn't mean that it is the best way. You don't have to run through this process by yourself; there are many reasons to involve the team. The benefits are particularly apparent for complicated jobs: more ideas, specialist contributions, motivating the team for the job and getting the team working together.

Once you have decided on the best course of action you need to produce a plan to implement it and then delegate if appropriate.

Stages or no stages?

Many tasks, especially project work, take a long time to complete. In order to keep motivation up, it can be useful to divide the task into stages. The completion of each stage has positive benefits for motivation. If a task is likely to last more than a couple of months then breaking it into stages that take roughly a couple of weeks each can be helpful in producing a job that is well done. In addition, weekly review meetings can help to summarize what has been achieved.

Identify resources

It is critical to identify accurately the resources required for the task. The main problems come in underestimating requirements – this can mean you come unstuck later. Either use an accurate means of identifying resources or add a safety margin of about 25 percent. Time is nearly always underestimated; again, add a safety margin. It is better to finish earlier than planned and impress your boss than be late and upset him or her.

Setting objectives

It is vital to write down a specific task objective, together with standards and time limits. This is so that you remind yourself, and later the team, exactly what has to be done. This should be a confirmation of your original objective in solving the problems or completing the task.

You now start the delegation phase. It is important that you now decide:

- Whether you are going to delegate the job or parts of it.
- Who you are going to delegate it to.

If the team is involved and the work has to be divided among them you need to set personal objectives for each team member, and agree these with them where possible.

Delegation in practice

...you can delegate tasks and authority. You cannot delegate accountability...

What should you delegate?

Initially, you need to decide whether or not you are going to delegate the job at all. The first question you have to ask, one that many fail to ask and a major cause of discontent and poor quality work, is: "Does any of my team have the time to take on this job at present?" Team members have individual abilities and may be able to complete the job within different deadlines, so to some extent the time allowed may determine who you consider for the job.

In reality the pressure of work most people are under means that you need to consider carefully who you give the job to. Many people tend to take on work if their boss asks them as a matter of principle – even if they don't think they can do it. In some cases this is because they are frightened to say no, in others because they want to create a good impression.

So you must be sure that the individual or team you delegate to has time to do the work. Where possible you should ask them. Even if they tell you that they have enough time you still have to take the decision as to whether or not you really think they can do the job. If people on your team always say they can even when they can't, you must ask why. Are they worried about how you might react if they say they can't take on the job? Are they capable of managing their own

workload effectively? Are they afraid of letting you down? Equally, if you ask someone to take on a new job and you think that they have time and are able to do it, but they don't want to, you need to know why. In either case, you need to sort out problems of this nature within the team so both sides know where they stand. How you agree the delegation of specific jobs with specific people will be covered later.

There are some tasks you should probably delegate and some that you should not.

Where possible you should delegate the following:

- ■ Routine and minor tasks
- ■ Tasks that other team members can do as well, if not better, than you because of their skills or knowledge.
- ■ Tasks that will develop the skills and knowledge of team members and may provide them with a challenge.

You probably should not delegate:

- Tasks that are outside the experience or knowledge of team members.
- Important matters that need your authority/experience to be completed successfully.
- Areas relating to your responsibility to build, maintain and develop your team.

Bending the rules

Occasionally, you may need to bend these rules. For example, if you are engaged in a new type of project, you may have to delegate some tasks to people who have no experience of it and help them build it up as they go along. If you have an individual you wish to develop he or she should also be given experience relating to the development and maintenance of the team.

From the general list above you can see that the degree to which a job is important and urgent has an effect on how you are able to delegate it. If a job is both highly important and extremely urgent you may not even be able to delegate it; if you can there may be few people on your team who can take it on. So you can also use the "importance/urgency" rating as an indicator of both whether, and to whom, you should delegate the task.

High and low leverage

You will also notice from the general rules that routine and ordinary jobs are easily delegated and those of a more complex nature, particularly those related to longer term activities and team development, tend not to be. This gives another general division that some people find useful – the idea of "high leverage" and "low leverage" tasks. Where possible low leverage tasks should be delegated and high leverage tasks done by you. Examples of the high leverage tasks are training, planning, gaining the commitment of others, motivating the team, setting up systems, setting and agreeing objectives and building and maintaining relationships. Most of these are longer term activities that ensure that the team is going to be effective in the future – they tend to be the proactive jobs you do. The day-to-day routine jobs are the low leverage tasks – generally reactive to something that has happened or needs doing. You should try to delegate the low leverage tasks to leave you time for the high leverage ones that guarantee the long-term strength of the team.

Some experts suggest that by effective delegation you should be able to spend 80 percent of your time on the high leverage tasks and 20 percent on the low – with many people the ratio is the other way round. Just spend a short while jotting down the jobs you do each week and think about which you really need to do yourself and those you could delegate.

Delegation in practice

Who should you delegate to once you have decided to delegate the job?

So you have decided that you need to delegate this job. The next question is who to and what delegation style should you use?

You need to consider two main factors when thinking about who might take on the work. Do they know about the job – in other words, do they have task knowledge and experience – and are they motivated and committed to doing it? These factors are important in deciding how you are going to delegate. If the person you ask to do the task knows nothing about it, they are going to take a lot more supervision than someone who has carried out similar work. The motivation level is also important. If they are highly motivated you know that once they have been told how to do it they can be left alone to get on with it. If, however, they lack incentive and initiative, you have to keep coming back to ensure they are still doing the job at a reasonable speed to finish it on time.

You can see from this that, if you keep your team motivated, the minimum benefit you gain is reducing the time you would otherwise spend checking they are doing the job properly and stimulating them to keep going.

You can also probably think of other combinations that you have met at work – the person who knows the job and is motivated, the person who knows an average amount but still needs help and the expert who is losing motivation.

An individual's working knowledge and motivation is directly linked to the amount of supervision required to oversee a task.

Classifications

It is therefore possible to classify people by their experience/knowledge and level of motivation/ commitment in relation to the job in hand. This gives you an indicator of the level of supervision required and also the delegation style you can use. Remember, a person may be an expert at a particular job but know nothing about another – so the classification applies only to a person and a specific job at any one time. Bear in mind that people develop over time as well!

Beginner

Beginners are new to the job in hand. They are generally highly motivated because they are interested in learning new skills, and your possible delegation of the job to them shows them that you give them credit for their skills. The only problem is that as they are new to the job they don't have much idea of how to do it. So they are high in commitment but low in task knowledge. While you probably won't have to put in extra effort to motivate them you will have to take time to show them how to do the job in some detail.

Learner

Learners have developed some job experience but are not fully expert. So they have medium task knowledge. They may have high, medium or low motivation – sometimes after an initial burst of enthusiasm on joining the organization their motivation can drop. In this case you can use the task knowledge they have to coach them through the job. If their motivation has reduced this coaching can also include encouragement to motivate them more. So the learner probably has medium task knowledge with medium motivation.

Regular

Regulars are even more familiar with the job than the learner, generally with medium to high task knowledge. However, sometimes you have to provide them with extra motivation because theirs is variable. When the motivation has reduced after some time in the organization the person is sometimes called a "plateaued regular" – you can probably think of people you know who are like this. Regulars need to be given "hands off" support. Then they can use their undoubted knowledge but have your support to boost their motivation. So the regular has medium motivation with high task knowledge.

Performer

Performers are probably the individuals you find easiest to delegate to – they have high task knowledge and are highly motivated: you can therefore delegate the task fully to them. This also allows you to give them much more freedom of action than others – however, it still allows you the option of having a system of reporting back during the task or contacting you if problems arise. Ideally, you want all your team to be performers, so that you can delegate what you need to with confidence.

The classifications to look at in detail are:
Beginner
Learner
Regular
Performer

Delegation in practice

Matching names to jobs

Think of those you work with – you will probably be able to fit most people into one or other of the categories below for the different jobs they do. You may find it useful to help you understand this to write down the names of five people you work with together with two of the jobs they do. Alongside write whether you think they are a beginner, learner, regular or performer in each area. To classify each just look at the level of task knowledge and motivation and match it to the classifications:

- Beginner – low task knowledge/high motivation
- Learner – medium task knowledge/variable motivation
- Regular – high task knowledge/medium motivation
- Performer – high task knowledge/high motivation

Which delegation style should you use for which individuals or teams?

To be fully effective as a manager you need to be able to match the delegation style you use to fit the situation you encounter. This allows you to:

- Give the correct degree of freedom/responsibility to the team or individual.
- Ensure the team/individual is not demotivated by oversupervision.
- Have the opportunity to develop the individual/team via the task if desired.
- Give yourself more time to work on tasks only you can complete.

Use of the best delegation style for the situation is therefore crucial. It also has the side effect of reducing many potential sources of conflict within the team.

In practice you can use any delegation style for any situation – either highly hands on (controller) or hands off (co-ordinator/facilitator), So it is possible to always use one style irrespective of the task or people involved. This is the trap that some managers fall into, often always being only controllers.

Finding a solution

It should be simple to choose a delegation style for any job. The problem is that only one particular style will be appropriate and bring out the best in the individual or team. The challenge is how do you find out which is the best style for all the different jobs and individuals you might ask to do them? This may seem daunting: if you add up all the jobs you have to delegate and all the people you could delegate them to. Even if you have only three team members and four jobs you already have 12 potentially different delegation styles required! A chief executive said that he once asked a former boss how best to choose a delegation style for different people. He was told: "Always delegate in an appropriate fashion; that is the secret." Sound and correct advice, but of little practical use – how do you know "what is appropriate"?

There is a simple, quick and effective solution that will give you a good chance of getting it right. Each of the delegation styles (controller, coach, consultant, co-ordinator) is most appropriate for differing situations. You need to learn which style best matches which situation.

The results of the Delegation Style Questionnaire on pages 24-27 will have given you an indication of the delegation style, or styles, that you use most and least often. You need to be able to use any of the four styles identified as each of them is the most effective for the sort of situations that regularly come up at work.

You will have no difficulty employing the styles you use most but you may have to practise using the others. But which do you use when?

We have already looked at classifying different people by their experience/ knowledge and motivation. The different types of people in the list above can be matched effectively with the different delegation styles that you can use. You can match your style to the individual or team by looking at their task knowledge and motivation. This works in practice as follows:

Matching delegation style to job
Each individual's experience and motivation for the job matches a delegation style:

- If a Beginner in relation to the job to be done – use the Controller style
- If a Learner – use the Coach style
- If a Regular – use the Consultant style
- If a Performer – use the Co-ordinator /Delegator style

Which delegation style should you use?

This provides a simple format for finding the optimum delegation style for the situation. When considering allocating work to your team use this simple format to determine the delegation level for the task in hand and it will help you to maximize your team's performance. It also ensures that your leadership style is matched to the job in hand. The degree of delegation, and so freedom to individuals, you give is closely related to leadership style. By getting the delegation right you are also probably leading in the best way.

Try to assess each delegation situation you face in terms of the style required by the task and then use that style. After a few months' practice you will find that you are able to do this effectively and more naturally, eventually without seeming to think about it. The development sections in the next chapter will take you through how to learn to do this.

The secret is to allow the team or individual the freedom to do what they are able to do and provide support to enable them to do what they cannot. In other words, give as much responsibility and support as you can. You should stress that coming back to you if problems are encountered is NOT a sign of weakness but effective communication. This allows you to be more generous with responsibility without the worry that things may "go too far".

The model above is not fixed but is just a guide to help you develop the habit of matching style to situation – there will be cases where you may be between styles and, in practice, the coach and consultant can be very close.

Agreeing style with team/individual

To gain an even better match, where possible, the style to be used should be discussed with the individual/team. This allows them to offer to take on more responsibility, should they feel they can cope with it. How you can be effective at doing this is looked at in more detail in the next chapter.

Remember that people develop over time

Keep in mind that a critical part of your role is to develop your team. This enables them to maximize their performance, keeps them up with technical and other developments and allows you more time for management work. Inevitably as they develop and can take on more responsibility you MUST change your leadership style and level of delegation. So, even for the same individuals doing the same task, as they become more experienced you MUST change your style, generally allowing more responsibility. This can occur within as little as three months, or even during a week away on a course. If you do not give them more responsibility the team will be frozen in time and will not be motivated or effective.

If time is short

In certain situations, time may be very short – for example, in emergencies. In such situations, although the best delegation style might be the consultant, for instance, you may not have time for this approach. In such cases, there is nothing wrong with using a more directive and less participative approach if something has to be done very quickly. In other words, make your mind up, tell people what to do and get on with it!

Having decided who to delegate to how do you implement the decision?

Now you have decided to delegate the job and who is going to do it you have to start the ball rolling. This includes selecting objectives, agreeing them where possible, briefing the team or individual about the job, checking on how it is going and carrying it through to a successful conclusion. Your delegating function is not over until the job is successfully completed. Some managers think that once they have delegated the job that's the end of it, but it's not. Remember: "You can delegate all the job but you can't delegate all the responsibility."

Some general principles

To help you reach a successful conclusion the next section gives you some general principles on the stages between the decision to delegate and the end of the job. This includes:

- Setting/agreeing objectives.
- Briefing the team or individual.
- Checking on how the job is going and giving feedback where necessary.
- General motivation of the team.

...Be available to give advice...

Determining their objectives

Ensure that your team understands:
The objective of the job and the standard of performance required and how this will be assessed.

Be specific
Once you have decided to delegate all or part of a job to someone you need to set them a specific objective. Otherwise they won't be clear about exactly what they have to achieve. This is most important – if they don't understand the goal they may do the wrong task, go about it in the wrong way or not finish it on time. There are some general rules for setting objectives:

- Objectives must be specific – individuals must know exactly what is required of them.
- Objectives should be understood and agreed.
- Objectives should stretch the individual and offer challenges but allow them to achieve.
- Objectives should be seen to be relevant to an overall strategy – they know why they are doing it and how it fits into the "bigger picture".

While it is possible for you simply to decide on the objectives yourself and then brief the team or individual, this is only effective for simple, routine tasks. For more complex tasks it is important that you agree the objectives with the person(s) who will do the job so that if they have any concerns about being able to complete it, you can sort them out before the start. Important issues to be resolved from the outset include:

- The resources they will be given for the task, including time.
- That they are responsible to you and should come back to you if anything they are unable to resolve arises.
- The amount of authority delegated – what they can and can't do without further reference to you.
- The target date or time for completion of the task.
- The reporting system: set one up if required, especially if the task is going to be a long one.
- That they can do their own thinking about how the task is to be performed – unless it has to be carried out in a particular way.

How do you express what you want done?

Briefing the team or individual

Briefing the team or individual is important. Most problems within organizations between people are as a result of poor communication – generally both parties having a different understanding of the same discussion. So to make sure that the job is done how you want you have to brief in a logical way. This ensures that you include all the information they need so that they can do the job. If you don't explain fully and the job doesn't get done at least some, if not all, of the blame is yours.

When telling a team or individual what you would like them to do many people leave out critical information. This is particularly true for the more complex tasks a team may have to do where team members all have different roles. The format in the box on the right will ensure that you include all the important information.

Briefing format

- **BACKGROUND** – why the task is being done and why the team or individual has been chosen.
- **OBJECTIVES** – what the team/individual has to achieve.
- **GENERAL TASKS** – the overall plan.
- **SPECIFIC TASKS** – stages, individual tasks if appropriate.
- **ADMINISTRATION** – where support is coming from, resources, interim reports, action on problems, contacts.
- **TIMINGS** – start, finish, stages.
- **ANY QUESTIONS?** – always ask if there are any questions.

Using this is simple: write "BOGSAT + Questions" down the side of a piece of paper. By each letter write the information listed in the format above. Once you have inserted all the relevant information you can then use this sheet to brief the team or individual. With an individual this briefing will be a personal "one-to-one" conversation and does not need to be formal, but the information above should still be passed on. When you are delegating to a large project team it is essential to brief in a clear and formal manner so everyone knows what to do.

How do you tell them what you want done?

BOGSAT explained

The **background** to the task is important and is often left out. People like to know why they are being asked to do the job, in terms of why it has to be done, why they have been selected to do it and how this fits in with the bigger picture. This gives you the chance to motivate them by showing that they are contributing to the organization and team and they have been selected because of their skills and knowledge: it demonstrates your faith in them. Explain all of this in the background section. The motivational value of this section is often underestimated. It is probably the critical part of the briefing process for motivating the individual or team. Leaving it out will reduce the chances of the task being successfully completed. The **objective** given in the briefing is specifically what is to be achieved by the end of the task. It is best expressed in a clear one line statement. For example: "Our objective is to increase the annual sales result by 25 percent."

The **general outline** section provides a brief overview of the plan to achieve the objective, for example: "We are going to increase income by targeting clients from the engineering industry sector."

The **specific tasks** section may include details of how the general outline is to be achieved or, in the case of a team task, what each team member is required to do. For example: "John,

I'd like you to research the engineering companies that currently do x, y and z."

The **administration** section covers anything that relates to the support needed to get the job done – where the resources are coming from, are there contact telephone numbers, who is doing the paperwork?

The **timings** section gives everyone full details of when things start and finish together with other relevant timings – possibly stages to be completed during the job.

Ask for questions

Make sure that you ask if there are **any questions**. This will probably be the last time you communicate before the task starts and if anyone is unsure about what is required it needs to be sorted out now. By asking for any questions you give anyone the opportunity to ask for clarification of points they may not fully understand and it gives you peace of mind, knowing that what is required is clear and unambiguous.

All this may seem highly formalized for just telling people what to do on a day-to-day basis – but it can be done quickly in a personal way for individuals or more formally for a team. You should always use this format to ensure you don't miss out any information the person you are delegating the job to needs to know. You can practise it by yourself by thinking of a task you might have to brief the team on and running through the headings to gain a feel for the format.

Using the format in practice

Even on a day-to-day and one-to-one basis this way of structuring information can be extremely effective: *"John, we have been asked to improve the turnround time for client queries by the MD as part of the overall quality improvement initiative. Because of your experience in this area I would like you to produce a report on how we might achieve an improvement. I need it completed by the end of the month and you can get all the information and typing support you need from my staff.*

You can offload your current projects to Steve to enable you to concentrate on this. It's up to you how you do it but if you have any problems or want advice you can come and see me any time. Is that ok? Have you any questions?"

It takes just 40 seconds to get this information across. All the information from the BOGSAT format is there. In practical terms a more detailed discussion would probably follow in which the job would be discussed in more detail, John maybe wanting more of an idea of possible approaches from the boss and the boss giving John the information he wanted to enable him to start the task with confidence. If John is really experienced and motivated he may well just say *"Yes, that's fine"* and start the job.

You can see that the delegation style you have decided to use now also determines the way you brief as well. So if John is a performer (motivated and with high task knowledge) then the briefing is as short as it is above – the boss would use the co-ordinator style. If however he is a beginner (motivated but with low task knowledge) at this task then the level of information the boss has to give will be much more detailed, to fit in with the controlling content that is required.

So while ALL briefings should include the critical information required by the person who is to do the job the more you move toward the controlling style the more you need to include detailed information to make up for the individual's lack of task knowledge. It's no good briefing beginners as if they are performers – they just won't know what to do. At the opposite end, if you brief performers as beginners they will think that you are treating them like idiots and become demotivated. So briefing style must match the delegating style. This may seem obvious, but there are many people who seem to change the style they have decided to use between the initial assessment and the briefing of the team or individual. If you decide to go "hands off" stay "hands off".

How do you monitor job progress?

Having delegated the task you need to ensure that it is all going to plan and that there are no problems. To do this you need "feedback" from those doing the job. This can be encouraged in a number of different ways. Feedback does more than allow you to gain an idea of the progress of the job; it can also give you other information that will make you more effective at your job if you use it.

There is a difficult balance to be struck between letting the person get on with the job and seeking feedback. In general you should seek feedback only at agreed times or stages. If however the person doing the job wants to give you feedback, encourage

Encouraging feedback from your team is important. It gives you:

- More information on how the job is going.
- Better quality information on how the job is going.
- Checks that what you asked to happen is really happening.
- Allows the person doing the job to tell you if they need help or there are things stopping them doing the job effectively.
- Allows you to understand the person doing the job better.

them at any time. This doesn't mean you have to hover about close to them waiting for the feedback – hovering bosses make people feel that they are being watched. They will come to you if they want to.

Getting feedback

Some people are worried about giving any information to their team leader. They may have had bad experiences in the past or feel that their views are not wanted. Many factors stop team members from giving feedback on how things are going or how they feel the job could be made to go better. The main one is how they view their boss. If your team aren't giving you feedback maybe they are worried about your response – make it clear to them that their feedback is valued by you. In some organizations the whole atmosphere discourages anyone, especially staff lower down the ranks, from giving feedback. However, it's not just managers who have ideas that can benefit the team and the organization. Indeed, one idea from a warehouse worker saved a computer company £8 million in one year! So encourage your team to give you feedback when they want to, not just when you ask.

Good feedback keeps the job on track and you up to date with what is going on – this information helps your delegation to be effective, motivates the

Feedback tips

- Actively encourage feedback – tell the team you welcome it.
- Use active listening skills – try to listen more than talk.
- Act on feedback – do something about what you are told.
- Tell them what is happening – this keeps the team in the picture and encourages them to tell you what is going on.
- Hold regular two way briefings – this keep the communication going.
- Build a team culture that encourages feedback.

team and creates a good team culture. Feedback should be via both day to day discussion with team members and, if possible team meetings held on a regular basis. These meetings can be very useful in enabling the person doing the job to report on progress and allows other team members to offer ideas and suggestions.

To help you get this vital feedback Active Listening and Open Questioning can be very effective.

Active listening

Before you start, find somewhere to talk where you will not be interrupted.

- Show interest in the person talking.
- Listen until they have finished.
- Use encouraging gestures.
- Show support – even if you disagree.
- Help them structure their ideas.

- Summarize and agree the main points before moving on.
- Try to understand their position.
- Listen to what they are *not* saying.
- Don't let personal views interfere.
- Relax! You will listen better.

Open questioning

Always try to use open questions – those where more than a plain "yes" or "no" is required. Start all questions with words such as why, what, when, where, who, how. For example:

"Do you think there will be any problems with this job?" The probable answer is a straight "yes" or "no".

"What problems do you think there will be with this job?" The probable answer is going to be more detailed – or at least encourage the other person to give you their feedback.

How do you give praise or criticism?

After the delegation of the job the team or individual should be busily engaged in completing it. Ensuring that the job is finished and executed successfully is still part of the delegation process. During this part of the job you will be evaluating how it is going. You may want to give feedback, either positive or negative, to the team or individual. You should certainly give feedback at the end of the job.

Think about how you would feel if you had been doing a job for three days and you had no idea of how the boss thought you were doing. This is one of the major frustrations of people on all levels in organizations: "I'm very rarely told how I'm doing, I'd rather it was bad than not knowing where I stand." How often have you felt that? Try not to let your team reach that viewpoint, by giving feedback on how they're doing.

Giving positive feedback

In particular, remember to give praise when it is due. Some managers even assume that as people are paid for doing their job they shouldn't expect praise as well! In fact giving praise where it is due is one of the most effective ways you can motivate people. The good motivator uses praise only when it has been earned. Praising merely to create a pleasant atmosphere simply cheapens it. Just saying "Well done!" is better than nothing, but you can make your praise even more effective by following the simple format below.

Tips on praise

When giving praise, stress the following:
- What was good about what someone did.
- Why it was good.
- What it says about the individual.
- The impact on the team/organization.

Good practice

In addition, remember that rewards are much more effective if people know in advance how they will benefit for good performance. Expectations and targets should be agreed by all the parties.

You will need to give those working for you feedback on their performance both on a day-to-day basis and in their formal appraisal. It is easy to demotivate individuals by approaching this in the wrong way – we are all inclined to be a little sensitive when our performance is being discussed. Giving feedback on a regular day-to-day basis is vital. You cannot keep all the feedback for the formal appraisal, though some managers try. Giving feedback just after the event is much more effective and allows suggested improvements or development of skills to take place at once, not six months later after the formal appraisal.

Feedback also helps team members to develop and improve their skills. Giving effective feedback is a critical part of getting the job you have delegated done and motivating the team and individuals in it. The following guidelines will help you to get it right.

Tips for giving effective feedback

- Pick an appropriate time and place.
- Be specific – either positive or negative feedback has extra value if referred to a particular example.
- Give feedback in a logical sequence (a) Measurable performance/facts. (b) What this says about the individual. (c) Consequences for the team/organization. (d) Any resulting actions that may follow.
- Never use gossip; always base feedback on facts.
- Feedback is aimed at helping the individual improve his/her performance, not an ego trip for the manager. Constructive criticism, not censure, is required.
- Check the individual understands what you have said by asking them.
- Even with negative feedback take a positive approach – how matters can improve, for example. Also take recent improvements into account.

Principles of giving feedback

Giving negative feedback

It's not just difficult to receive negative feedback; giving it is hard for many people, too. If you follow these steps the process will be less unpleasant than it can be. It is never something you will enjoy, but you must do it if required. There is no point putting it off or not doing it; the problem, or the damage caused, will only become worse.

- Explain why what you are about to say is important.
- Be specific and use examples.
- Describe what happened first rather than judging. For example: "You didn't make the deadline and as a result the client was unhappy."
- Concentrate on specific skills or actions that can be improved or changed.
- Agree future action to prevent a repeat of the problem.
- Don't put off giving negative feedback – sort it out as soon as possible.

Even though you might not like giving negative feedback, you have to – not just because it's your job, but because the team wants you to! It may sound strange that people may want you to tell them that they aren't doing well, but it's true. At the start of this section on feedback you were asked to think how you would feel if your boss doesn't tell you that your're making mistakes because he doesn't like giving negative feedback. So what happens? You carry on as before, the job isn't being done properly, your boss isn't happy with it but won't tell you – a recipe for even more problems in the future for everyone in the team.

Just by taking a few minutes to tell you that the job isn't being done properly, how he can help you to do it right and then to help you develop solves all the problems – you know where you stand, you understand more about how the job should be done, you have improved your skills, the boss is getting the job done correctly and doesn't have to keep checking up – everyone wins. In fact it's probably more important to give good feedback on problems than give praise – but try to give both !

After the job is done – the review

That's it, the job is finished, no more to do. In fact there is one last step that is nearly always forgotten but which is highly important for the development of the team and making sure jobs go well in the future – the Review.

After every job you do, even if it's only you involved, review what went right and what went wrong. Just on a scrap of paper write "what went well" and "what could be improved" It will take no more than five minutes. List under each the parts of the job that fit into each category and then use those in the "what could be improved" category as areas to improve performance in the future.

It is very easy to extend this to simple jobs done by other people on your team – even if you don't actually get involved in the work yourself. At the end of each job get their feedback by asking what went well and what do they think could be improved . This will only take a few minutes, but the benefits can be substantial – new and better ways of working, increased motivation because you showed you valued the individuals opinion and the increased chance of more feedback in the future.

It is also possible to get each team member to do the process themselves for each task they carry out to help themselves think about the jobs they do.

If they have any good ideas then they can pass them onto you. If you can build a culture where everyone considers all the jobs they do and looks for ways to do better your team will improve in leaps and bounds. Feedback is essential in complex team tasks where you may not see everything that is going on. Someone may have noticed a point that you need to know about. They may not even realize that it is important, but you need to have this information and the end of task review is the ideal place to bring everyone's thoughts together.

While it is still fresh in people's minds, ask each of them to report how their part of the job went and if they can think of any way it could be improved. Team leaders who try this are normally surprised by the number of good ideas that emerge.

If there is no single large task to review, then have a regular team meeting to discuss how the normal multitude of small jobs went that week. Again, experience shows that ideas to help improve performance often come up at such meetings.

Delegation and motivation

In getting the job done, effective delegation is a critical skill and will help motivate the team or individual. But it also applies in reverse – if your team is motivated, delegating is easier. Motivation is a critical component in assessing which delegation style to use. As a general rule, the more incentive there is to work the less time you have to spend keeping an eye on the team to ensure that the job is being done.

There are some simple principles of motivation that you may find help you in your work with others. Abraham Maslow, one of the leading experts on the subject, said that we all do things for a reason. This reason can be put down to each of us wanting to have or achieve certain things. We will work to be able to satisfy our needs. This was put forward in his "Hierarchy of Needs", below.

Abraham Maslow, Hierachy of Needs (1964)

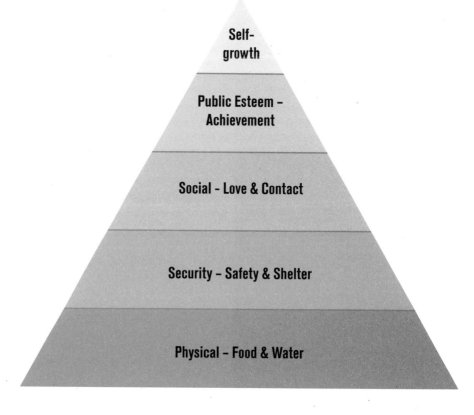

Self-growth

Public Esteem – Achievement

Social - Love & Contact

Security – Safety & Shelter

Physical – Food & Water

The model explained

Each of us, Maslow said, will work to answer our needs for food and water, safety and security, love and social contact, public achievement and self-growth. Generally, once we have satisfied the lower needs we move up the pyramid to the higher ones. Assuming that most of your team have the lower needs satisfied – food and water, safety and shelter, love and social contact – then it is the two highest needs that they will want to satisfy: public achievement and self-growth. This is how you can motivate them – by using their desire to gain approval from yourself and their peers and to grow as a person by developing their skills, experience and self-respect.

By giving individuals the opportunity to achieve recognition and develop via the jobs you delegate to them you will be able to motivate them.

Here is a checklist of practical steps you can take to create and sustain an environment that will motivate your team. Some of these relate to delegation and some to other skills. If you can provide all of these you will make sure your team is fully motivated.

■ Set challenging targets, but make sure they are realistic and achievable. Try to involve people in determining their own objectives. People need to feel in control.

■ Make sure your team is fully informed about decisions that will affect them and anything relevant that is going on in the company.

■ Involve more people in planning work and/or innovating.

■ Increase individuals' responsibility by delegating more. Allocate work in such a way that everyone has a chance to take on more responsibility and gain more expertise.

■ Allow people maximum scope to vary the methods, sequence and pace of their work. Remove as many controls as possible while making sure that everyone knows who is responsible for achieving defined targets or meeting standards.

■ Make it clear that what people achieve or fail to achieve is up to them.

■ Make sure that the relationship between effort and reward is clearly defined.

■ Recognize achievements, but don't cheapen praise by dispensing it too freely.

■ All of these steps link back to the principles Maslow put forward; by using them you will motivate your team, develop their skills, be a more effective leader and create a positive team culture.

Delegation problems: you

Why some people, including you, might feel nervous about delegating:

You may feel nervous about letting your team make decisions or do tasks that will reflect on you.
In the end, you can't do it all alone. There will come a point when you have to delegate, and it's best to do it when you want to rather than having it forced on you by events. Effective delegation can make your life so much easier – you will have more time and the team will be more motivated. Look at the list you completed earlier of jobs that you do each week – you must be able to find one or two that are not critical that you could delegate almost at once. If you are really worried start by delegating a few routine jobs, see how they go, practise your delegation and then move on to bigger tasks.

You may feel that you are more competent than your team members.
You may well be more competent in many task areas, but that doesn't mean that the team is incompetent and can't do any of the jobs. Again, if any of them can do one of the jobs you should delegate it – it will give you more time for the tasks that only you can do. There are also other reasons for delegating even if you are more competent – people develop by learning new skills and this can only

happen if they are given the chance to try things they have not done before. This is the process we all go through when we learn to drive a car – going from the inexperienced to the experienced. Using the classifications for delegating introduced earlier – moving from beginner to performer – you should try to get all your team to be performers at all their jobs but if you don't let them have a go how can they learn and improve?

Even if they have never done the job before you should encourage one of your team to try it – if you are the only person who is able to do the job what happens if you are ill? If you think about it, it makes sense to have a team made up of people who can do a number of different jobs so that the team can be flexible to match various jobs as they come in.

So even if you are more competent, you must ensure that the team members develop their skills so they become competent as well. The best way to do this is by agreeing a development plan with each team member – this is covered later in the book.

You may find it difficult to analyse tasks to decide if, and to whom, to delegate.
If you look carefully at the ideas put across in this book and follow them through logically you should be able to

determine quickly and simply which jobs you can afford to delegate and who is the best choice of person to delegate them to.

You may be afraid that the team expects you, as the manager, to have all the answers.

In delegating to them you are admitting that you cannot do without them – the team does not expect you to be an "all-knowing hero".

In the complex world of modern organizations no one, not even the chief executive, knows everything. The minimum you must delegate is the tasks where members of your team know more than you. Remember you are there to manage the team, not do all its jobs; they are different functions. Most teams want you as their boss to delegate to them: it shows that you respect their skills and experience. If you don't delegate it may demotivate them.

Solving delegation problems

Problem	Solution/reason
You feel nervous about delegating.	Delegate small, simple jobs to start and build up.
You are more competent than the team, so why delegate?	1. You can't do it all. 2. They need to develop their skills. 3. Delegating improves motivation.
You're not sure what to delegate.	Match individuals' skills and experience to the jobs in hand – use the formats already introduced.
You think you're supposed to know everything.	No one expects you to know everything – the role of the leader is to use the skills and resources of the team as effectively as possible – not to do all the jobs that come in!

Delegation problems: them

Why do some people not want you to delegate to them? (And how you can overcome this)

Most people want to be given more responsibility – but a few don't. In some cases they just don't want responsibility for whatever reason and forcing it on them is a waste of time and a potential disaster. In most cases where someone says they don't want the responsibility there is a reason under the surface. Once it is revealed, it can be overcome. If you think they can do the job but they don't, you need to find out what the problem is and solve it. You need to air a problem that is restricting their taking on responsibility and thus reducing their, and the team's performance. Here are some of the most commonly encountered problems with suggestions for solving them.

They are worried about the consequences of failing.

You need to boost their confidence and offer them as much support as they think they need while doing the job. You will have found yourself that once you get into a job what seemed daunting at the start is in fact easier than you thought. Start with small simple jobs and build them up slowly to more difficult ones. Assure them that they will have your support and that you are sure they will succeed.

They lack confidence in their own ability (similar to the first problem).

Again, encourage them to take on small jobs first and then build their confidence by increasing the size and complexity of the task. Make sure that you give them all the support they need, especially in the early stages.

They find it easier to ask for the solution than work it out for themselves.

If time is short you may have to give the answer to get the job done on time. In most cases they should work through it themselves. Explain to them that if they want to develop and take on more responsibility they need to practise their skills by working through tasks. In taking the short cut, they may reduce their chances of future career development or success.

They think that managers are there to take responsibility and not delegate it.

You need to explain that each team member has to share part of the load and that the team can only be effective if everyone contributes. Focus on their expert skills and experience and say that you need these qualities to help the team achieve objectives.

By asking them to contribute in this way you should be able to overcome this problem.

They feel no loyalty to the organization.
If this is the case, how much loyalty do they feel to you? If there is some degree of loyalty to you, but not the organization, you still need to find the cause of the problem and solve it. If there is no loyalty to you either then the problem is more serious – it is even more important that you find out why, talk it through and try to resolve it.

They disagree with what is being done.
There is an obvious problem here and it needs to be discussed and solved. Why do they disagree with what is being done? Again, find out the reason, talk it through and resolve it.

They think that they are not going to receive sufficient reward for their efforts.
You need to establish what reward they think is fair for their work. Are they being repeatedly asked to do unpaid overtime? For them to feel exploited something must be going wrong within the team or organization. This is another problem that needs to be explored and solved by agreement.

If individuals don't want you to delegate to them how do you deal with it?

- Offer of delegation by you.
- Rejection by them.
- Discuss with them the rejection to discover the reason. Use active listening and open questions. Don't just reaffirm the delegation.
- Address underlying problems.
- Confirm with them if their problems have been addressed.
- Discuss and agree delegation at appropriate level.
- Offer on-going support.

Delegation pitfalls

There are traps that managers often fall into when delegating, so you need to learn how to avoid them, or at least get out of the trap once you recognize you are in it.

Always delegating to the most capable – understandable, and an easy way out

It gives you the security of knowing that virtually nothing can go wrong. The only problem is that it doesn't do much for team development. What happens if the capable individual is ill or even leaves the organization? Carefully look at each job you have to delegate, rather than always giving it to the individuals who can easily do it. Is there another team member who would improve their skills if they were asked to do it? You can always enlist a capable team member to help the less experienced one with the job. This will benefit both – one gains job skills, the other coaching skills.

Delegating directly to your subordinate's staff without asking

By going directly to junior staff you will upset any plans that your subordinate has made. The job may seem urgent or more important than those they are doing, but you should always delegate to your subordinate and allow him or her to delegate to their team. They know the team better and will do a superior job at delegating. Even if, by chance, you think you are better acquainted with the team, it is still not the right approach. You wouldn't like your boss telling your team what to do without telling you, would you?

Failing to delegate tasks you enjoy doing but which others could do

Taking on tasks which are not essential for you to do is a classic problem for many people, especially technical experts. You have to let go of those jobs that you enjoy, but a team member could do instead. Many of these jobs tend to linger from when people were more junior. Sorry, but if a team member can do it let them. You must concentrate on the jobs only you can do. And if the team sees you keeping the enjoyable jobs you are probably giving them some bad ones – which is not good for morale. In the end your function is to do the jobs you need to, not the ones you like.

Delegating tasks which you should do but which you don't like

There is no excuse for this. We all have to do jobs we don't like if they are our responsibility; even if team members can do them, we should do them. Bite the bullet, do the job and reward yourself for a nasty job well done. Your team will respect you much more for doing this than palming the job off onto one of them.

Perfectionism

In many areas of work there are certain functions or activities that require perfect completion. Within these specific work areas you may find it difficult to delegate to those that are not fully task competent. However, many people fall into the trap of assuming that all task areas require perfect completion.

By assuming that perfection is necessary across the board, you restrict the degree to which you can delegate. This is particularly true when you have inexperienced team members. The problem is you need to bring them to the point at which you are able to delegate, yet you cannot risk allocating work to them to help them develop because of the requirement for complete accuracy. You can achieve complete accuracy where required by providing close supervision, either by yourself or a more competent member of your team, but there are many areas where perfection is probably not required.

An example of this problem is within the City of London where many organizations have a legally binding requirement for certain activities to be completed perfectly. Managers in these areas often tend to assume that all other tasks have to be completed to the same level and so find themselves unable or unwilling to delegate. They spend more time than they should supervising staff who may well be perfectly capable of doing the job and who would benefit by being able to develop their skills if they were given the opportunity.

Striking a balance

If you operate within an area where some of your work requires a perfect completion, the answer is to determine which of the tasks really do require perfection and which do not. Simply write a list of the major jobs that you and your team finish each week and mark those that have to be completed to perfection for whatever reason; this will then give you an indication of which tasks you may be able to delegate to members of your team who are not fully competent but who need to develop their skills in these areas.

For anybody who has to delegate and wishes to develop their team this is one of the most difficult balances to strike: between allowing people to develop and make mistakes and the requirement to produce perfect work. It will vary from situation to situation but try to make an effort to allow team members to take on the challenge and develop themselves, even if it does make you feel nervous. If you have given them the correct amount of support, then they should only have to ask for your assistance when they encounter problems.

Problem people you may have to delegate to

Shirkers

There are possible solutions to those who don't do their fair share of the work. Tell them that you have a problem, how you see it and then ask for their help in solving it. Suggest that the workload on the team means everyone must contribute and their skills and experience are a valuable asset. If possible, delegate work specifically to them. In co-operative teams the shirker can get away with it – it is only if you become more directive about their jobs that you find a solution.

Remember:
- A positive approach to handling problems and people is critical.
- Keep cool and try not to see these people as problems or enemies.
- Bear in mind what they contribute to the team.
- Think about how you can manage a way round or compensate for problems.
- Think how you could help them meet your needs and theirs.
- Do not react defensively or aggressively to objections.
- Respond constructively – show you see the value of what has been said.
- Produce a suggestion or, better still, ask for one to solve the problem.
- Aim for a "win/win" outcome.

Buck passers

Try to minimize their responsibilities; if in their eyes it's always someone else's fault, use factual information and job specifications to define their area of responsibility. Be positive about their involvement and contribution and ask them to contribute more. As with the shirker, if necessary, be more directive about what they do.

Pessimists

They always take the negative view and can demotivate others. If they come up with objections ask them how they would solve the problem they have just raised. If you can persuade them to find solutions they will generally give it a go. Encourage them to be positive and join in with the successful team activities. While they don't block the delegation process they can affect the success of the outcome.

There may be other problem types you find obstruct your delegation. Whatever the scenario, there are some ground rules that will probably help you at least to manage the situation, if not solve it.

If problems persist

If all else fails, you are in charge, and if necessary to complete the job insist that it is done in the way you ask. This should be a last resort after as much discussion and attempts at negotiation as time allows; but occasionally some people just have to be told what to do. That is part of your role, and unpleasant though it may be, you have to grit your teeth and do it. Most people who push you to this point do not expect you to be firm, but think you will give in – that is why they are doing it. Don't give in; stand firm and tell them what you want done.

- Deal with the problems promptly – they only get worse with time.
- Plan what you want to say before you speak to the person.
- Focus on facts and consequences.
- Try to find the cause of the problems – active listening and questions.
- Check you have really understood what they have said
- Agree a course of action
- Be positive and look to the future. Your objective is to help them perform better, not to chastise or insult.

Critical Points – Chapter 3

Make sure you are planning for the job that really is the one that needs doing.
Decide what to delegate based on the ability of your team, not what you want to do.
Consider the job knowledge and motivation of each individual for each job. This determines if they are a:

BEGINNER
LEARNER
REGULAR
PERFORMER

Then match your delegation style to this:
Beginner – Controller
Learner – Coach
Regular – Consultant
Performer – Co-ordinator
Agree the style where possible.

Brief them using:
Background
Objective
General outline of job
Specifics of job
Administration
Timings
+ Any questions?

Set clear, realistic and achievable objectives.
Give and request feedback while the job is underway.
Constantly motivate the team.

Delegation exercise

Here are a selection of delegation situations you are likely to meet at work. The exercise is designed to give you practice in using the format introduced earlier.

Tick each of your choices and, when you have finished, look at the answers at the end. You could also try to work out which style each answer represents.

___

1 You have just taken over running a team which has to implement a new system quickly. The team has been working together only a couple of months and has not made good progress. This seems to be because it does not know clearly what its objectives are and how it should achieve them.

What would you do?

a) Ask for their suggestions, then decide the action plan yourself.

b) Clarify the objectives, and tell each of them what to do.

c) Sit down and talk to them, helping them work out the best solution.

d) Give them the opportunity to work out the best course of action themselves.

| a | b | c | d |

___

2 An experienced team member has had some good ideas on tackling a problem, but isn't sure about what to do next.

What would you do?

a) Choose the best solution yourself and tell her what to do.

d) Help her to work it out for herself and produce a plan.

c) Discuss her ideas and then tell her how to do it.

b) Give her the time and space to work it out for herself.

| a | b | c | d |

___

3 A member of your team has developed considerable knowledge in one specialist area and your team has to do some work in this area.

What would you do?

a) Agree with him what he should do, and leave him to develop the correct approach.
b) Ask for his ideas, but tell him how you want it done.
c) Tell him in exact detail how you want him to do the job.
d) Listen to his thoughts and help him to support other team members during the job.

| a | b | c | d |

---

4 You lead a young and keen team, but they are failing to meet some deadlines.

What would you do?

a) Allow them to sort out the problem themselves.
b) Tell them what needs to be done and how, then supervise it.
c) Listen to their ideas as to how they can meet the deadlines and help them to implement them.
d) Discuss the problem and tell them how you want them to put matters right.

| a | b | c | d |

---

5 You have given some of your team a difficult job. They are competent but have not previously done this job before. They have come up with some good ideas but don't know how to take things forward.

What would you do?

a) Listen to their suggestions and help them make a decision.
b) Let the group work it out by themselves.
c) Decide what should be done yourself and tell them.
d) Ask for their suggestions but make the final decision yourself.

| a | b | c | d |

Delegation exercise

6 You have been promoted and are taking over an experienced team that has been working well with little supervision.

What would you do?

a) Allow them to get on with the job as before.

b) Discover how they do things and give them encouragement to continue.

c) Tell them they have done well and then announce what changes you want to introduce.

d) Tell them how you want them to do the job.

| a | b | c | d |

7 You see that one of your more experienced staff has problems in achieving one of his targets. He had done excellently up to now.

What would you do?

a) Ask for his ideas, but decide on what to do yourself.

b) Let him work it out for himself.

c) Support and encourage him, but let him decide what to do.

d) Decide what should be done and tell him.

| a | b | c | d |

8 You have been keeping an eye on a new team member. She is becoming both more experienced and more confident. You want to develop her further.

What would you do?

a) Praise her for her efforts so far and let her have more responsibility.

b) Leave her to decide how to do the job on a day-to-day basis.

c) Continue to keep a close eye on her.

d) Explain how she should do things in the future and give her encouragement.

| a | b | c | d |

9 You have given an experienced but unenthusiastic member of your team an important job to do. He seems to be struggling with some part of it in which he lacks previous experience.

What would you do?
a) Allow him to get on with it by himself, as you had with previous jobs.
b) Ask him about his ideas and, if necessary, explain how he should do it and help him plan it out.
c) Tell him his skills are valued and involve him more to motivate him better.
d) Act quickly and firmly to urge him to improve his work and watch him closely.

a | b | c | d

10 A new member has just arrived in your team. She is keen but has no relevant experience of the fairly complex task you want her to do regularly.

What would you do?
a) Explain what she has to do and then show her how to do it?
b) Ask how she might tackle the job, but show her how to do it?
c) Help her work it out for herself?
d) Leave her to work it out for herself?

a | b | c | d

11 Your team are highly professional and feel the need to make some changes in the way matters are done to improve their performance in routine activities.

What would you do?
a) Help them work out the best solution and then support them as they implement it.
b) Ask for their suggestions but make the decision yourself.
c) Let them decide how best they can make the improvements.
d) Tell them what they should do and supervise the implementation.

a | b | c | d

Delegation exercise

12 A new member has recently joined your team and has been making good progress over the past year, but now seems to be less motivated that when she arrived.

What would you do?
a)   Let her decide how best she can get the job done.
b)   Explain what has to be done, ask for her ideas, but take her through step by step.
c)   Help her to work it out for herself.
d)   Tell her exactly what you want her to do, and supervise her closely.

| a | b | c | d |

These are the best styles for each of these situations:

1b	5a	9b
The Controller	The Consultant	The Coach
2d	**6b**	**10a**
The Consultant	The Consultant	The Controller
3a	**7b or c**	**11c**
The Co-ordinator/ Facilitator	The Co-ordinator or the Consultant	The Co-ordinator/ Facilitator
4d	**8a**	**12b**
The Coach	The Consultant	The Coach

The Styles

Situations	Controller	Coach	Consultant	Co-ordinator
1	b	a	c	d
2	a	c	d	b
3	c	b	d	a
4	b	d	c	a
5	c	d	a	b
6	d	c	b	a
7	d	a	c	b
8	c	d	a	b
9	d	b	c	a
10	a	b	c	d
11	d	b	a	c
12	d	b	c	a

Exercise conclusion

This exercise will have helped you practice choosing the correct delegation style for differing situations at work. If, in addition to just trying to find the best solution in each, you also tried to identify which style each possible answer related to, this will have been even more useful.

In practice, some people find the distinction between the coach and consultant tends to blur. The difference is that as a coach you provide advice on a more proactive basis (when you think it is needed), whereas as a consultant you provide advice on a reactive basis (when the person doing the job asks for it). But on a complex job, both styles may be needed as you work through it.

The controller and co-ordinator style are more easily defined in practice. The former imposes strict supervision, the latter likes complete delegation of the job.

4

Delegating more tasks
Developing your skills
Planning development

Choosing which jobs to delegate

Matching your style to the team

Identifying your strengths and weaknesses

Building your development plan

What jobs could I delegate?

This section is devoted to helping you improve the way you delegate by practising the theory. To gain maximum benefit it is important that you complete all the exercises in the section. They are not complicated and will enable you to build on the self-assessment that you have already done and to help you plan how to improve your skills.

The exercises you do will help you to:
■ Decide which of the jobs that you currently do could be delegated.
■ Make sure you use the best delegation style for the jobs each of your team does.
■ Work out how to do this in practice.
■ Think how to put together a development plan to help improve your skills in the future.

To improve your skills you need to assess how you are doing at present. The self-assessment questionnaires earlier on will have given you an indication of how things are going, but to improve as much as possible you need to be able to assess your own performance day to day and week to week.

To make sure this happens effectively, follow a simple process. Each time you do a job observe what you do, afterwards record how it went, then evaluate what was good and what could have been done better. This seems simple but few of us do it. It doesn't have to be a large report – just a few notes on a piece of paper of what happened and ideas for improvement. It will take you about five minutes – well worth the time. Some people find that jotting down ideas for self or team improvement in a desk diary, if you have one, is safer than slips of paper that tend to go astray.

What jobs could I delegate?
As you have seen, both in practice and from earlier sections of this book, many people hang on to jobs that they could easily delegate. The first step in the program to improve your skills is to recognize which jobs these are and to think about who could possibly do them. You can call this the "What jobs I could delegate list". You need to be honest to complete this successfully – as with all the other exercises in this book, if you cheat you are only cheating yourself.

To produce the "what jobs could I delegate list" write down the 10 jobs that you do regularly each week on the left hand side of the page. Then place five columns to the right, the first headed "name", the second "without training" and the third "with training", the fourth "training details" and the fifth "time saving". An example of the layout of the list is on the opposite page.

Consider each job you have placed on the list. Is there any member of your team who could be delegated part or all of that task either straightaway or with some short term training? Be honest, don't cling on! If there is, write them down in the "name" column next to the relevant job. If they could take responsibility at once tick the "without training" box or, if they require some short term training, tick the "with

training" box. The "training details" is to give you an indication of how long the training may take to raise the person to the right level and who will do it. Will it be you, more experienced team members or will you send them on a course?

Finally, indicate the number of hours each week that this task takes you and therefore the number of hours saved by delegating it.

"What jobs could I delegate list"

Job	Name	Without training?	With training?	Training details	Time saving
1. Weekly sales figures	Peter Smith	Yes			2.5
2. Liaison with minor clients	Ann Richards	No	Yes	Two weeks shadowing Andrew Thomas	1.5
3. Sending out information to clients	Bill Dobson	No	Yes	John B to teach him – about a week	(2.5 to John B)
Total					4.0 Me 2.5 JB

What jobs could I delegate?

When you have run through all the regular jobs you do, see which you could delegate and add up the total time that could be saved. However, remember that you can only delegate if they have time to take on the extra responsibility.

You will probably have found that you can delegate about 10 percent of your total workload – if the figure is lower you need to delegate more; if it is much higher either you are working effectively or you aren't being as honest as you should be!

You can do this exercise on a regular basis – possibly annually or every six months – because as your team develops they learn new skills and build up experience, so in time you should be able to allot more tasks to them.

This exercise can be particularly useful if you have a team made up of some experienced members and some inexperienced ones. Can the more experienced members act as controllers or coaches to the newer members? You can therefore extend the list, as in example three on the previous page to re-allocate jobs done by more experienced staff to more junior ones – but ask them first.

This list will have given you an idea of the tasks you presently do but that you could delegate. Use it to help you allocate these jobs to the respective team members.

Am I delegating in the right style for my team members and their jobs?

What about tasks that you already delegate? Are you delegating effectively by using the right style for the situation? In practical terms, do you give the person performing the task the maximum responsibility that they can take for that job. If you aren't, as we have seen earlier, you may be wasting time and demotivating them by over-supervising them. We all tend to over-supervise, even if it is only because the individual was inexperienced at first and we haven't realized that they can now do the job in hand without our constant guidance.

To make sure you are maximizing the responsibility of your team members (in technical language, "empowering" them), you need to think about the delegation style you use for each person for each specific task. You will recall from the previous chapter that the key to effective delegation is the ability to match the delegation style to the individual or team for each job they do. To develop your skills you now need to analyse closely the style you use at present on every occasion.

The reason that you do it for each individual is that some people are excellent at some tasks and not at others. You can probably think of a job that your boss does that you could probably do without supervision but others for which you would need support. The same principle applies to your team. So you may need to use a different style even for the same person depending on the job in hand. This sounds fine in principle but getting it right in practice is more difficult. You know you should do this but in practice you just don't have the time to think about it – or that's the excuse most people use.

Remember that each team member will fall into one of the following categories for each job they do:

- Beginner – low task knowledge/high motivation
- Learner – medium task knowledge/variable motivation
- Regular – high task knowledge/medium motivation
- Performer – high task knowledge/high motivation.

And also which delegation level was appropriate for them:

- Beginner – Controlling style
- Learner – Coaching style
- Regular – Consultant style
- Performer – Co-ordinator style.

So as a general rule the greater the job experience and motivation the easier to delegate, as you can become more "hands off".

Using the format you can now write out a list of all your team members and the main jobs they do with a note of the classification (beginner or whatever) based on their motivation and knowledge/experience.

This will form the basis of your Team Delegation Style Assessment in a later section.

Name	Job	Classification

Suggestions for improving your delegation styles

Through this book you have discovered that you need to use a range of delegation styles to maximize the performance of your team and you will have identified the styles you use most often. So to improve your delegation skills you should develop the ability to use the styles you are not experienced at using – your weaker styles. If you refer back to the self-assessment in Chapter 2 you will see which of the styles you are weakest at using; note down on a piece of paper which these are.

The following section will give you suggestions how you can improve your skills in using those styles. If you feel hesitant as a controller then, when you have to delegate in a situation that needs that style, refer to the suggestions below next to "controller". If you follow them you should find that it works better than before – and all you have to do is practise using the style. Getting the styles right is a case of having practice, practice, practice. In the end you will be doing it right without even thinking about it.

To improve your effectiveness in each style	
Controller **(Direct control)**	Be more directive. Give clear objectives with standards of performance and deadlines. You should determine how the job is done – use close supervision. Intervene if required.
Coach **(Encouragement/Supervision)**	Work more closely with individuals, taking them through each job; suggest ideas but allow them to try to do each stage, intervening if you think you should.
Consultant **(Close support)**	Explain what the job needs to achieve, ask for their ideas and suggestions, let them decide how the job is to be done with your support. Be on hand to give support if they need it.
Co-ordinator **(Hands off with support)**	Be more "hands off", let them decide how to do the job and to get on with it. Leave them to come to you if they need help. Keep in contact but leave them to take the initiative.

The best use of different styles: a summary

You may find it useful to think about the benefits and risks that using the different styles may incur. This chart sets out the main factors that you should consider:

When you use these styles keep an eye out for the first signs of risks building up and deal with them immediately. So use the benefits, but watch out for the drawbacks.

Style	Benefits	Risks	Example Situation
Controller	Rapid decisions if time is short, clear objectives and performance requirements. Little chance of any deviation from what you want done – fewer potential mistakes.	No involvement from individual/team, possible lack of commitment. No team development or initiative. Takes a lot of your time.	For people with little experience, especially on critical jobs. Where time is short. Don't forget you can delegate controlling to more experienced team members if appropriate.
Coach	Helps build confidence as people learn, minimizes risk of mistakes but encourages them to take responsibility.	Can be time consuming depending on how fast they learn. Can leave individual dependent on you.	When people have some experience but still need a fair amount of support. Possibly where motivation is flagging.
Consultant	Reduced time spent by you. Builds commitment and encourages taking on of responsibility. Team members can suggest ideas and improvements.	Decision-making process may take longer. Team can expect to be asked all the time.	For those with more experience who are capable of contributing ideas and who don't need you at hand to get on with it. May need your help if complex problems arise.
Co-ordinator	Gives you maximum time to do other tasks. Team able to get on with job themselves – builds innovation, motivation and commitment.	May end up with a group of individuals not a team. .	For the motivated and experienced who are capable of getting on with it and solving most problems that may come up.

Finding out the right delegation style for each member of your team and the jobs they do

To maximize everyone's performance by ensuring you use the right delegation style you need to complete a Team Delegation Style Assessment – this is simply a form on which you write the name of each team member and next to it the four jobs they do on a regular basis.

You already have the basis of this from the previous section on classifying team members in different jobs. For each job you write if they have high, medium or low task knowledge/ experience, and also if they have high, medium or low motivation to do the job.

	Team member's name	Tasks (4) that they do regularly
1		
2		
3		
4		

Analysis

This then will allow you to write down which delegation level the format suggests is the best from the four possibilities. You can also record what style you have been using in practice.

Does the suggested best style match what you were doing in practice? If it doesn't, then were you over- or under-delegating in the workplace?

A form to show you how best to lay out this analysis is below.

You will notice that the form also includes an "agreed" column – this is covered in greater detail in the following section.

Knowledge/ experience?	Motivated/ committed?	Current style used	Possible future style?	Style agreed ?

How can I further improve my team delegation skills?

Having done a style assessment you now have a general idea of the delegation style that you think is best for the individual and job. But don't just go ahead and tell them; if you have time you should think about agreeing the style with them – hence the "agreed" column in the table, to tick when you have done so.

You will have found that if you talk to team members you probably get a better idea of what is going on than if you just guess yourself. It follows that this may also be true about the best delegation style to use for the individual concerned. This may worry some people: a team leader asking how the subordinate would like to be delegated to – the stuff of anarchy!

In fact, those team leaders who have tried this are still in their jobs and most of their teams are performing better than before. You make the final decision about how you delegate, but receiving an input from the individual can be helpful.

The benefits of this process are:

- It gives the individual the opportunity to offer to take on more responsibility.
- It gives you the information you need to determine the best delegation style.
- It motivates the individual because you are consulting them.
- It helps establish the objectives of the job and ensures that both sides understand and agree them.
- It allows any possible problems that the individual might foresee to be dealt with before the job starts.

The best way to approach this seems to be: explain to the individual/team that you wish to maximize their effectiveness by giving them as much responsibility as they are able to accept. Discuss either the job in hand or, if doing a delegation assessment for the first time, the three to five main work activities that they are engaged in, and ask if they think the delegation level is right. Ask them if they would like more responsibility – where possible the style agreed should encourage the individual to take on some form of challenge that will enable them to develop further, such as learning new skills as responsibility is increased.

In practical terms it is probably better to do this with a copy of the style assessment form rather than purely verbally and from memory. Then agree with them the most effective delegation style for each of the jobs they regularly undertake. This you will use for the next few months. As individuals or teams develop you will need to update this agreement on a regular basis – not just at appraisal time.

Increasing responsibility

You may find it useful to discuss this informally on a quarterly basis to see if the individual or team is ready to accept more responsibility; an individual can greatly improve their skills within a three-month period if they make an effort or have attended some form of training. Use this to update your "What jobs could I delegate list" (see page 71).

This is the point at which you can also discuss with the more experienced team members the possibility of them acting as supervisors to the inexperienced staff. This includes encouraging them to delegate simple tasks to the newer members so that they can concentrate on the more complex jobs – exactly the same principles as you are using.

Other general development suggestions
Role models/ mentors

Many people have found that a role model or mentor can help them develop their skills profoundly. First, what is the difference between the two? A role model is another individual whose behaviour you copy because they take what you think are the right approaches. They may be successful and you might wish to emulate them. This can be effective if they do things right. A word of warning: be sure that you are not copying poor behaviour and always remember you are not a clone of another person. Always adapt what they do to your own style. If you don't your team will detect the change fast and resent the fact that you are putting on an act. The role model will possibly not even realize that you are copying their example.

In contrast, a mentor works with you to give you support when you need it and help you find your solutions to your difficulties. They will be in touch with you to help you to find solutions to your problems, so you can access and use the mental assets of a more skilled and experienced person, saving on the time they took to gain that level of knowledge themselves.

How can I further improve my team delegation skills?

Finding a mentor can be one of the most effective of all forms of development, especially when combined with the self-analysis and development planning of the type covered in this book.

If you are given the opportunity to work with a mentor who you respect and who can give you the benefit of their experience and skills, grab the offer with both hands. If your organization sets up a mentoring scheme and asks for people to join, give it a go!

If your organization does not have a mentoring scheme or there is no one inside the organization prepared to help you, you may be able to get some support from a more experienced person from outside. Even if they are not fully conversant with your organization or business sector they may be able to help you find solutions to your problems. A good mentor is able to help those from many organizations as the principles of best practice apply everywhere. Professional bodies, management organizations and business schools may be a source of good advice. Reading to improve your knowledge in your weak areas is also very effective.

Other suggestions

Here are a few general tips that may be useful in helping you develop your skills.

■ Think about your relationships with those you work with (the team, boss and peers). Are they open and positive working relationships?

■ Remember the importance of a positive approach to problems and problem people.

■ Anticipate problems from team members, peers or bosses; ensure you tackle problems early, before they have gone too far.

■ Don't be afraid to seek help from trusted colleagues or a mentor if needed.

■ Don't rush into anything – always take a logical approach, using the ideas and suggestions in this book. It increases the chances of doing it well and reduces the risk of a disaster.

Putting together a development plan

Understanding how you learn

All of us learn throughout our lives by having experiences and analysing what happened as a result – as a child you quickly discovered that if you touched something hot it burnt you and subsequently you didn't do it again. Although more complex, the principles of how we learn at work are the same.

The way this works is as a learning circle:

Having an experience

Reviewing the experience

Learning from the experience

Planning the next steps (development plan)

Long-term planning

This book is designed to help your learning circle, both as you read it and then as you go on to put together your plans and improve your skills. You have gained the necessary experience through your work, reviewed it during the self-assessment, learnt from it and are now moving on to planning your development. Don't think that this is a "one off" that you do only while reading this book. To develop your skills fully you need to use this circle every time you can. The best way is to produce a development plan now and review individual experiences/jobs briefly as they happen. Then, six monthly or annually, sit down, assess yourself and write out another formal development plan for the next period.

If you want the best results you can use this book to help in your self-assessment and planning on a regular, day-to-day basis.

You may also have realized that, according to the time-honoured phrase: "You need to know what you know and what you don't know to get better." The self-assessment section will have helped you discover some of this, but there may be more.

Development action plan

To find out what you need to do to improve, you must know what you need to improve. A model called the Johari Window (below) can help you think about this more clearly.

The model suggests that there are four areas of information about ourselves that exist – we need to know all of them to understand how we might progress.

The easy information is what others know about you – "public knowledge" – and what you know about yourself – "secret knowledge". However, there is some other information that you may need to have to build on your present abilities in more difficult areas – what others know about you but you don't know – "own blind spot" – and the information that no one knows – "unknown at present". This may at first sound a little strange, but if you think about it this is what happens in practice. Have a look at how you arrive at the information in the two more difficult areas.

The "own blind spot" contains information about you that you don't know but others do – for example, if you have ever found that you have a habit such as scratching your ear or nose while talking – but you don't realize you do it. It comes as a shock when someone tells you what you do!

Anyone who has been on video during a course or exercise will remember that moment when such habits – such as saying "er" at the start of each sentence – reveal themselves. So other people see quirks in you that you may not be aware of.

Information known to others	1 **Public knowledge**	3 **Own blind spot**
Information not known to others	2 **Secret knowledge**	4 **Unknown at present**
	Information known to self	**Information not known to self**

Blind spots and feedback

Knowing what is covered by this blind spot is essential to the way you work with people – especially when delegating. Discovering the blind spot emphasizes the great importance of receiving feedback on your progress, not just from yourself and your boss, but even from your team. They are the people who see you in action so they can tell you if you have habits that you should know about because they affect the team, the individuals in it and their performance. These can be little points which people find upsetting that you don't even think about. Just recall a boss you may have had who regularly made comments about a team member working more slowly than others or always delegating the nice jobs to one person – you may not even realize that you are doing it. So the answer to discovering this information is seeking FEEDBACK from those you work with.

The other section – the "unknown at present" – is information that neither you nor others know. It is even more difficult to uncover, and it can only be done by you working at some form of self-analysis or discovery. This all sounds a little psychological and intimidating but in practice it is not. You will have discovered during your life that you are good at something you had never even thought about before – maybe not even related to work but based on a hobby or similar activity. You discovered this either by pure chance or, more likely, you had some idea lurking at the back of your mind that you might like to try that.

Discovering what is in this hidden area is the same. You probably have an idea about how you work with people, what you do well and what not so well, but possibly behind it is another area that explains this. You may not like doing certain jobs or feel intimidated by certain people – which or who and why and what causes it and what can you do to solve the problem? You may become deeply depressed when things don't go well – why and what causes it and what can you do to solve the problem? The answers to these are probably in this unknown area. If you can think searchingly about such problems, analyse them and try to find the causes then you will find the answer and be able to tackle them.

Personal development planning

Identifying your strengths and weaknesses

Consider how well you do at each of the following areas, the main areas you need to get right to delegate effectively, and the main areas covered in this book.

Assess yourself and put a tick in the box that indicates your current level for each of the skills listed. The chart below will show you the areas in which you feel your skills are either good, satisfactory and need improvement. These need to be built upon to produce a specific plan to develop each skill that needs working on.

If time permits, you can then also improve the skills classified as satisfactory to be good – after all, why just be satisfactory at something if you can be good at it?

Personal Development Needs Assessment

How are your skills at:	Good	Satisfactory	Could be better!
Working out exactly what job I have to do			
What jobs should I delegate?			
Who should I delegate to?			
(matching job to skills/experience)			
Identifying Beginners - Performers			
Determining objectives?			
Telling people what they have to do – briefing.			
Use of Controller style			
Use of Coach style			
Use of Consultant style			
Use of Co-ordinator style			
Getting feedback on how it's going			
Praise and criticism? – giving positive and negative feedback.			
Holding an end of job review process ?			

Improving your performance via skills development

- Assess your skills.
- Identify strengths and weaknesses – i.e. where improvements are needed
- Produce a detailed plan to turn each weakness into a strength with:
  a. Objective
  b. How it will be done
  c. A deadline.
- Get your managers support where possible.
- Initiate the plan.

The above table shows the practical steps you need to take to improve your present skills. In previous chapters you will have assessed yourself, thought about how to get it right, looked at what you do at work at present and thought about how you can develop via learning.

The table on the previous page will have focussed on the areas in the delegation process and considered your strengths and weaknesses. Thus you are now ready for part three of the process – producing a detailed plan to turn weaknesses into strengths.

Depending on how hard you have assessed yourself you may have found that there are a lot of "could be betters".

The secret of getting the best out of development is to focus on those areas that you think you are weak and then, when they have been improved, move on to those that aren't quite as bad.

On the list on the previous page highlight the three areas you think that need most improvement – generally the areas that are most problematic at work. These are the ones to address first. The next stage is to produce a draft development plan for each weakness before putting it onto the development plan form – writing it out in draft helps you think about it. Write out each problem area, shown by the "could be better", at the top of a separate page and then under each, list the problems you have in that area. Then, using the ideas from the book, list the steps you could take to reduce these problems.

So, if the plan is to "solve ABC problem", the steps you need to take to achieve this are, for example, "more practice at ABC", or "set up a meeting with team members". Also put in a realistic deadline for each. If you think that you could benefit from support or help from your manager or organization also include that.

You should now have all the components for that specific weakness to be addressed in your development plan and these can be inserted onto the form on page 87.

Development action plan

To produce a development plan simply take each of the skills where you ticked the "could be better" column and photocopy a "development needs" (there is one opposite) for each.

Then write in under "development needs" what the skill is. When you have done this for all of the skills in the "could be better" category, do the following: if any of the actions you propose would be more effective with support from your boss or the organization as a whole, then include the actions they could undertake to help you in the sections "actions by your boss" and "organizational support?". This could involve discussing with your boss how they may have dealt in the past with problems similar to the ones that you now face.

Set a deadline

You must set yourself a deadline to have completed your actions by – and stick to it. If you don't, there is always something that needs doing instead and you will suddenly find that it is two years down the road, you've done nothing and as a result someone else has been selected for promotion. Remember it's up to you to develop yourself: no one else will do it; a good boss may help, but in the end it's up to you.

Checklist:

- Write out exactly what the skill is that you need to improve. This may be "need to take more care in delegating to more experienced staff – tend to use the wrong style – too controlling."
- Write out the steps you need to take to improve this in the "actions by you" section. This may include actions such as: fully assessing an appropriate delegation style before giving out jobs, attending a course, completing a team skills summary to see who can do what, holding meetings with team members to discuss their views on taking on more responsibilities or seeking a mentor. Each action you undertake should fit in with a specific area that needs improving. It may not just relate to time at work – you could benefit by reading a book on an appropriate area in your spare time as well.
- Write in if your boss or organization could help you to improve in this area.
- Put in a "to be completed/ achieved by" date.

Development needs:

_____

_____

_____

Development needs should include technical training, management
competencies and any skills you may need to develop for the future.

Actions by you:

_____

_____

_____

Actions by your boss:

_____

_____

_____

Organizational support?

_____

_____

_____

To be completed/achieved by:

_____

_____

_____

Immediate action plan

You may find that the "development needs" action plan tends to identify improvements that may take some months to be effective. To keep you motivated to develop yourself you should try to achieve something as quickly as possible. You may find the format below useful in this. It is an Immediate Action Plan – something that you can implement straightaway.

The first two suggestions are already included based on the formats we have looked at earlier – so there are two tasks you can do at once. Just add on other improvement ideas from your list of "could be better" that can be done almost at once, such as "practise using consultant style more" or "seek feedback on my performance". The introduction of regular team meetings can also be implemented almost at once.

If you can find at least five improvement actions to take immediately, including the two already written in, then both you and the team will show an immediate benefit. The team will be more motivated and encouraged by your improvement. Don't delay; do it today – an old phrase but still true.

List 10 steps you will take within the next month to improve the performance of your team by effective delegation.

1   Discuss most effective delegation level with each team member. Encourage them to take on more responsibility.

2   Discuss personal development plan to improve my delegation of the team with my manager and initiate. Explain the support I would like from them to help me achieve my objectives.

3   _____

   _____

   _____

   _____

4   _____

   _____

   _____

5

6

7

8

9

10

Developing your team

The techniques of delegation that you have already seen will hopefully match the present skills of all your team members. However the workplace is not static and individuals and teams constantly need to develop new areas of expertise to meet the challenges of the future. This may be as a result of technological developments, changes in legislation, new systems being introduced or other factors which demand that the team and individuals within it have new skills. Even on a day-to-day basis some members of your team will inherently be more skilled than others.

If you find that a particularly able individual is due to leave the organization, you need to develop the abilities of another team member to take their place or a skills shortage will exist within the team. As a result, you may suddenly find yourself having to do work that you previously delegated. This can even happen on a day-to-day basis when team members are ill or on holiday.

Extra challenges

It is essential for you to develop the knowledge and motivation of team members so that in the future they are able to take on more responsibility than at present. In a perfect world you should aim at having your team made up entirely of "performers". By careful use of delegation you can successfully develop the ability of your team members. Where you delegated at a certain level, maybe to a learner, and you use the coaching style, consider the possibility of using the consultant style and allowing them more responsibility.

This may provide them with an extra challenge that enables them to develop further. Refer back to the chart you completed on the delegation styles; you can use for each of the task areas your team members function in. You can probably identify individual areas for each team member where you may well be able to move your style one stage further toward the performer.

If you think this is possible you should agree this with the individual and try it in a safe situation. This may increase the chance of a mistake being made – by choosing a safe situation the risks are minimized. Making genuine learning mistakes is a critical part of the development process.

The ceiling level

Although most people wish to take on more responsibility, as the level increases you may find that some individuals become reluctant to take on more. This may be for some of the reasons considered earlier and these need to be discussed with the individual so that any underlying problem can be solved. Otherwise their potential for development will be severely restricted.

Remember you can pass on the principles of effective delegation to the more experienced team members so that they can start to delegate their simple tasks, with your approval, to the newer individuals.

Asking someone to take on the development of another individual is one of the highest compliments you, as their boss, can pay them. It shows your faith in them and can improve their performance greatly as well.

Team development checklist:

■ Explain to the team what you propose and how it will develop and benefit them.

■ Get them to assess themselves in all areas of their job: where do they feel they need help ? What are their personal goals?

■ Make your own assessment of each team member.

■ Discuss with each individual their general future and development in particular – use open questions and active listening.

■ Agree a strategy:
(a) Which skills to improve
(b) How to do it (including help from you)
(c) Deadline

■ Write it down in the Development Plan format you used and each keep a copy.

■ Have regular meetings to check on how they think it's going (not just at appraisal time – every three months is a good rule).

Helping your boss to delegate to you!

We have looked at how you can be more effective at delegating to your team – but that is only part of the picture. The other half is the way your boss delegates to you. So enabling your boss to delegate effectively to you will also make life easier for both parties.

Yes, your boss probably doesn't understand you, doesn't communicate effectively with you, doesn't delegate effectively to you and so on... it happens to all of us. If, however, you stop blaming the boss and think about it logically – your boss has a boss, so is your boss being delegated to effectively or not? What problems does the boss have? Do you see the whole picture?

Looking through your boss's eyes

You need to help your boss to help you. If he or she is worrying about what your team is doing, he or she will probably be pestering you to make sure everything is OK. If you can show that you are a performer then your boss will feel more relaxed and become more hands off. Your relationship with your boss is nearly as important as that with your team, so you need to spend time getting this one right as well.

You can use the ideas in this book to discuss with your boss how he or she can delegate effectively to you. You need to sit down and talk through the best way for you both to do well. In the language of negotiation you need to find a "win/win" result.

Help your boss to be right – give the information needed and stick to deadlines. Take a positive attitude to your boss – respond positively even if you are not convinced and talk it through. Prepare ground for discussions in advance so you both know what is on the agenda.

Consider that your boss has problems too – see the whole picture, not just your own concerns. Don't give your boss nasty surprises; talk through problems in good time to avoid firefighting. If there is a difficult job to do, once agreement has been reached with your boss defend the decision as yours – even if you don't really want you team to do it.

Most problems with bosses are the result of the two people involved not communicating effectively with each other – you and your boss are a "team" as much as you and your team. You need to work together as such. This isn't a separate issue from your effectiveness at delegating to your team – if you and your boss work well together it will allow you more time to work with your team and you will have more support.

These issues can be discussed with the boss when you meet – as in your immediate actions plan – or discuss your longer term development plans.

Mistakes

You probably worry about people making mistakes and taking the flack yourself from above. Some would say that if you act as a controller all the time no one can make mistakes – but you would also have no time for your own jobs and your team would be totally demotivated. If you correctly assess the ability of each individual for each job and, where appropriate, confirm it with them the chances of mistakes are minimized.

Mistakes help people develop – so if you want someone to develop give them a job where they can make a few errors. Think of a couple of jobs you could give to these individuals where this is possible.

Conclusion

Effective delegation is all about knowing how to draw the best out of the people you work with – they work with you not for you. Give them respect and treat them as you would wish to be treated.

Whatever the pace and pressure in the modern workplace, one timeless principle holds true: Fail to honour people, they will fail to honour you (Lao Tzu, 6th century BC).

Critical points – Chapter 4:

Make sure you are getting it right by:
- Assessing which jobs you could delegate.
- Completing Team Style Assessment form and discussing the results with your team.

Develop your skills via:
- Assessing your delegation skills – this shows you where you need to improve.
- Getting feedback from others.
- Building a Development Action Plan and Immediate Action Plan.
- Trying to find a mentor.

Develop your teams skills via:
- Getting them to assess their skills.
- Helping them build their own development plans – to cover all their job skills, not just delegation alone.
- Supporting them in carrying through their development plans.

Index

Further reading

The contents of this book are one of the most detailed available on how to be effective at delegation, so it is not possible to refer you to books that go into even more detail. If you want to improve your skills in other areas, the other titles in this series will help. The books listed below will help you understand how delegation fits in with other critical skills you need as a team leader, or how your organisation works. There is a brief description with each.

1. The Management Task – Rob Dixon (Institute of Management Foundation, ISBN 0750606711)
A short book covering the basics of management. A good introduction to the subject. 120 pages.

2. Understanding Organisations – Charles Handy (Penguin, ISBN 0140156038)
A more in-depth look at how organisations work, covering not only the critical management areas, but also the more complex ideas such as culture and change. 400 pages.

3. Management – James Stoner & Edward Freeman (Prentice Hall, ISBN 0131087479)
A major book on the whole subject of management and organisations. May seem heavy and intimidating but a very useful reference to dip into if you are serious about management. 630 pages.

4. Management & Organisational Behaviour – Laurie Mullins (Pitman, ISBN 027361598X)
A very detailed book on management and how people function within organisations. Like the previous book, useful to dip into, rather than read all at once. 800 pages.

You may be able to get more information about management topics from the following organisations:

Institute of Management: 01536 204222
Institute of Personnel and Development: 0171 971 9000

The internet can also provide a good source of information on specific topics.

Printed and bound by Chorus-France